CORPORATE FAMILY MATTERS

CREATING AND DEVELOPING ORGANIZATIONAL DYNASTIES

by Drs. Steve & Rebecca Wilke

Corporate Family Matters: Creating & Developing Organizational Dynasties
Copyright ©2010 Drs. Steve and Rebecca Wilke
All rights reserved

Cover Design by Gary Christensen
Interior Design by Pine Hill Graphics
Editor Hannah Selleck

Publisher's Cataloging-in-Publication Data
(Provided by Cassidy Cataloguing Services, Inc.)

Wilke, Steve (Stephen D.)

    Corporate family matters : creating and developing organizational
dynasties / Steve & Rebecca Wilke. -- 1st ed. -- San Diego, CA :
LEADon Pub., 2010.

      p. ; cm.

    ISBN: 978-0-615-35775-1
    1. Corporate culture. 2. Organizational behavior. 3. Leadership.
4. Management. 5. Organizational effectiveness. 6. Personnel
management. I. Wilke, Rebecca Lynn. II. Title.

HD58.7 .W524 2010
658.4/092--dc22   1010

Printed in the United States of America.

The ability to deal with people is as purchasable a commodity as sugar or coffee, and I will pay more for that ability than for any other under the sun.

John D. Rockefeller

Table of Contents

Preface

Every business is a corporate family. It doesn't matter if your company has ten employees or ten thousand; the relational bonds within the organization are very similar to those in the basic family unit. Executive leaders who guide the company are like parents: setting expectations, developing skill sets and habits, checking progress, and rewarding good effort. And all employees experience varying degrees of sibling rivalry as they look to the "parents" for instruction and guidance, strive to meet expectations, vie for attention, and even test limits.

In over two decades of leadership development, LEADon has never met an organization that didn't qualify as a corporate family, though not all have recognized this reality. Those companies who have embraced the concept of "family" are way ahead of their competition in terms of productivity, profitability, and legacy. Why? Because your Corporate Family matters! If you and your employees feel united and committed to "the family," then you'll work harder to keep those bonds strong. When team members understand and respect one another, embrace and celebrate differences, and encourage each other to fulfill specific roles and responsibilities, then everyone wins—especially in the long run.

And long term success is what we're aiming for in *Corporate Family Matters: Creating & Developing Organizational Dynasties*. We want you and your company to not simply survive—we want you to thrive! Our goal is to help you create and develop a work environment that allows the men and women on your organizational chart to feel at home, inspiring loyalty and extra effort to maintain the productive atmosphere. As we offer new strategies to improve the relationships of your Corporate Family members, you'll be able to build High Performance Teams that will positively impact the bottom line. Most importantly, we'd like to assist you in leaving behind not just a business, but an organizational dynasty with a lasting legacy.

Acknowledgments

We appreciate all of the corporate family members with whom we at LEADon have had the opportunity to share our insights about leadership over the years. Your willingness to accept us into your corporate families for a season has added richly to our personal and professional development. We thank you all from the bottom of our hearts.

We are very grateful for the support of our family and friends who have been our greatest blessings in life. Much love and thanks go out to Teri, Craig, Mark and Julie who've cheered us on over the years and provided more support than we deserve. We would also like to thank Dana Dodds and Mike Bowling, exceptional businessmen and encouraging extended family members, who believe in LEADon principles and what we're striving to accomplish.

Finally, we offer our sincerest thanks to you, our readers. You continue to give us a reason to put pen to paper—in order to pass on the legacy we hope to leave behind for the next generation.

Chapter ONE

Welcome to the Corporate Family

Family life! Who shall fathom thy depths? Who shall declare thy meaning? How shall I compress into the few words I may permit myself any idea of thy sacred import?
Friedrich Froebel, "The Family"

When you enter any business, you should find a group of people working together with a shared purpose to fulfill a set of objectives. Whether the business is a bakery, a bank, or an international investment firm, all members operate within their unique culture, depending on each other to uphold responsibilities and looking to the "head" for direction. By definition, a family is a group that has commonality, typically comprised of parents and their children. In a sense, every business is like a family—we call this your "Corporate Family."

Think about that for a moment. "Family" means your office or jobsite isn't just a place to make money, and the men and women around you are more than mere employees. As strange as it may sound, your company is composed of a group of people with a common purpose, bonded together by your unique culture, hopes, desires, plans, and goals. The executives of the business have roles and responsibilities quite similar to parents, while non-executive employees look to these men and women for leadership, assistance, support and encouragement—just like children in any family setting.

> In its essence, a corporation is really about the body of people comprising it rather than the business product or service, or even the bottom line.

While many tend to think of business, especially corporate business, as tough, competitive, and focused on the bottom-line, this concept of family offers leaders a unique perspective. The term corporate comes from the Latin word, *corporare,* which means to make into one group. In other words, rather than consisting of a bunch of individuals doing their own thing, a corporation joins people together into one, united entity. In its essence, a corporation is really about the body of people comprising it rather than the business product or service, or even the bottom line.

This family perspective is exactly what we at LEADon believe will not only make your business stronger, but it will also provide long-term satisfaction and significant success to everyone involved. We've seen the positive results in hundreds of companies across the country. When leaders change from a "bottom line only" approach to one that addresses the needs of a corporate family, productivity and profitability increase. As employees start to view one another as part of the same family, becoming aligned, attuned, and committed

> When leaders change from a "bottom line only" approach to one that addresses the needs of a corporate family, productivity and profitability increase.

to each other, their emphasis changes from competing with each other for recognition to defeating the competition with a cohesive effort.

So how can you change your current corporate culture to one that encourages a stronger sense of family among colleagues and coworkers? First you need to understand a few things about families. You—and everyone in your company—are part of three types of families:

1. Your Family of Origin
2. Your Family of Procreation
3. Your Corporate Family

All of us are impacted every waking minute of the day by these three families! The five-star, twenty-four carat leader/employee/family member must understand this reality in order to fully develop personally and professionally. It's essential to understand the good and bad—the blessings and burdens—from the Family of Origin, Family of Procreation, and Corporate Family that simultaneously influence our daily lives.

> It's essential to understand the good and bad—the blessings and burdens—from the Family of Origin, Family of Procreation, and Corporate Family that simultaneously influence our daily lives.

Your Family of Origin is represented by the type of family in which you were reared. Many people are brought up in a traditional family unit, with a mom, dad, and their children. Others come from single parent homes, possibly due to divorce or death. There are also many people today who have been raised in blended families in which parents have remarried, brought together children from previous marriages, and even added additional children to these families. Also, there are kids who have been in foster care settings, orphaned, or raised by grandparents. No matter what our backgrounds, our Family of Origin impacts who we are each day. Blessings and burdens come from those early experiences in our Families of Origin, influencing both our personal and professional lives.

> **Blessings and burdens come from those early experiences in our Families of Origin, influencing both our personal and professional lives.**

Each of us also has a Family of Procreation—the family that either we are making currently or one we dream about making some day. If you are married, your spouse is part of this family unit. If you become a parent, children not only increase the size of this unit but also add to your responsibilities. Some Families of Procreation are created, broken, and created again. Divorce and remarriage are part of a cycle for half of the Families of Procreation today. In fact, because of this pattern, some relational experts have said that America has become a society of serial monogamists! You and every member of your Corporate Family have various experiences from Families of Procreation, which add to the blessings and burdens all of us carry to work each day.

> **As working professionals, we are part of a Corporate Family.**

Finally, as working professionals, we are part of a Corporate Family. For some, this unit may be small in size, feeling more like a traditional family. Many of us are part of large companies and even larger mergers and acquisitions, which means that your sense of belonging may only be to your branch or region in the business.

Interestingly, we spend most of our productive hours in our Corporate Families. Monday through Friday, from early morning until evening, we work by, talk to, and plan with our colleagues and coworkers. These relationships and interactions, as well as the problems they can create, are crucial components of our entire family picture, yet they are far too often overlooked in our hectic, overloaded schedules.

Often, we attend seminars, read self-help books, talk to pastors, priests, or rabbis, consume medication, and get therapy in order to deal with the struggles in our Families of Origin and Families of Procreation. Yet when we think about our businesses, how much time and energy do we invest in creating and developing a sense of family? If more effort was placed on improving your Corporate Family, how might initiatives and objectives be met on the business plan this next year? If leaders (parents) made an internal and intentional effort to improve unity, encourage trust, increase accountability, and reward positive outcomes, how much more would employees (children) strive to meet and even exceed expectations?

> Interestingly, we spend most of our productive hours in our Corporate Families. Monday through Friday, from early morning until evening, we work by, talk to, and plan with our colleagues and coworkers.

As a leader, you might be thinking: "You know, I didn't sign up to parent a bunch of adults. I have my own problems at home." We agree. We're not telling you that you need to rear more children, but your position as leader in some ways is undeniably similar to that of a parent of any given family. To avoid this natural aspect of your role and responsibilities could be more detrimental than you realize, affecting today's bottom line as well as your eventual legacy.

Employees look to their leaders to one degree or other like they did their parents. While many of them are highly skilled, exceptional professionals, their basic desire for guidance in the corporate family is similar to children. Most strikingly, because of the current status of our American culture, today's work-force comprises some of the brightest, but most dysfunctional people in our nation's history. This is partly due to the struggles in so many Families of Origin and Families of Procreation during the past several decades. From broken homes to latch key kids to postmodern morality, leaders are faced with the responsibility to fill in the gaps for their corporate family members as no other generation of leaders has had to do before! These gaps include self-esteem, character, motivation, discipline, and interpersonal relationships.

This need to provide more hands-on leadership to current employees is supported by LEADon surveys of executives in various professions. Many leaders report that most of their days are guided by the 80/20 rule. This means that 80 percent of their business day is spent solving problems involving their staff, while the remaining time (only 20 percent) is devoted to their area of expertise. Reflect for a few minutes on how you spent your time during the past several days. Is the 80/20 rule all too familiar?

> From broken homes to latch key kids to postmodern morality, leaders are faced with the responsibility to fill in the gaps for their corporate family members as no other generation of leaders has had to do before!

While you may not feel that you signed up for the role of "parenting" your employees, we must honestly tell you that it is yours. And if you don't find a way to fill in the deficits with your Corporate Family members, they will keep struggling and suffering, which will only cause your bottom line to struggle and suffer. On the other hand, when leaders take the initiative to improve their corporation's sense of family, people flourish. Not surprisingly, so do productivity and profitability!

Before we share more specific insights about your Corporate Family, we'd like to give you an example of a business that learned this critical lesson and dramatically improved its corporate legacy in the process.

Evergreen Systems* contacted LEADon several years ago to help improve its overall morale and business strategy. Starting in the Pacific Northwest, Evergreen had grown from a local business to a large corporation located in six, western states.

After several weeks of working with executives and their team at the company's headquarters, we were asked to facilitate a meeting with a large group of field and labor workers who the leaders considered to be "the problem children." Kurt Hanson, the new CEO, hoped to create a different culture at Evergreen, especially among these family members. He wanted them to feel more connected to the corporate family and less like nameless employees working in the field.

So at 5:30 a.m. one Monday morning, we entered a hotel banquet room where tables had been arranged for our meeting, and a buffet-style breakfast awaited the field workers. Soon these employees arrived, most in plaid shirts, jeans, and steel-toed boots. They entered warily, getting coffee and food before taking their seats.

It didn't take long after introductions were made to determine that these men (no female employees were in this particular cohort) were more than unhappy to be present. They wanted to be working, not wasting their time with some "suits" who'd come to lecture them on the company's latest plan for improvement. After talking through the issues that upset them (which included some heated dialogue), we were able to explain the leadership team's desire to improve the working environment

---

* many of the names have been changed for confidentiality

for all employees—beginning with them. We shared the company goal of becoming more of a corporate family instead of a conglomeration of companies, and we explained what this sense of family could do for everyone's personal and professional satisfaction.

By the time the meeting ended two hours later, most of these men met us at the door with smiles on their faces. For the first time in years, they felt appreciated by "corporate." While much work still needed to be accomplished in rebuilding relationships, Kurt Hanson and the leadership team of this company had made a good start in reconnecting with vital members of the corporate family.

> Due to the internal and intentional efforts of Evergreen's leadership, this company is headed toward becoming an organizational dynasty that will leave a lasting legacy.

While we were writing this book, the United States was in the midst of one of its greatest financial crises. Yet Evergreen Systems remained stronger than ever, both corporately (as a family, not just a business) and fiscally. They've weathered some rough economic waves, but Evergreen has survived when some of their competitors have not because the leaders changed the company's destiny by putting the "family" first. Due to the *internal* and *intentional* efforts of Evergreen's leadership, this company is headed toward becoming an organizational dynasty that will leave a lasting legacy.

We'd like nothing more than for this to be your story too. Let's look at some initial steps to ensure that your Corporate Family truly matters.

FAMILY TIME

This section gives you and your Corporate Family members a chance to reflect on the content of the chapter and apply the information to your specific circumstances. Look for opportunities to follow up on these thoughts in the days and weeks ahead.

1. Do you believe that everyone's Family of Origin, Family of Procreation, and Corporate Family play important roles in your workplace? Give some positive and negative examples.

2. How have your Family of Origin and Family of Procreation influenced your professional performance? Discuss them with other people in your sphere of influence. In the workplace, how can you overcome any negative experiences that may affect your work?

3. Does your Corporate Family have an intentional strategy in your business plan to improve the performance of all Corporate Family members? Can you explain how it works for everyone on your organizational chart?

Exposing Corporate Family Secrets

All happy families resemble one another; every unhappy family is unhappy in its own way.

Leo Tolstoy, Anna Karenina

Every family has its share of secrets. Some of these secrets may be good things that are kept quiet due to humility, or they may have been forgotten, like a late war hero or philanthropic relative in your lineage. On occasion, people aren't even aware of the "secret" until someone discovers old documents in the attic or shares a story at a family gathering. These kinds of secrets are some of the blessings that families should celebrate and share with the next generation.

Unfortunately, many of our family secrets aren't pleasant. These secrets are the burdens we carry to work each day from our Families of Origin and Families of Procreation. And, of course, there are Corporate Family secrets in our organizations that we deal with as well. Even if we may not be able to identify all of them, we sense that there are some lurking about—proverbial skeletons in the closet.

We intend to open and clean out the corporate family closet in this chapter. As an exceptional leader, you can no longer afford to ignore the problems, pressures, and pain that clandestine issues inflict upon you and your Corporate Family members.

> We intend to open and clean out the corporate family closet in this chapter.

You must *assess, diagnose,* and *treat* the specific secrets in order to develop a Corporate Family that works as a healthy, highly-functional unit to meet your business goals.

In order to begin this process, you need to understand that all families—personal and professional—fall somewhere along a continuum that runs from mild dysfunction to extreme pathology. Notice that perfection is not on this scale because it is impossible when you deal with real people living in the real world. *Problems are part of every family portrait, and no one is perfect.* Remember, we enter each of the families we discussed in Chapter 1 with imperfections, carrying the blessings and burdens of our experiences through life. And even if we are striving to be the best that we can be, real life hits us with difficulties and dilemmas that must be addressed to avoid more distress and dysfunction.

> You must assess, diagnose, and treat the specific secrets in order to develop a Corporate Family that works as a healthy, highly-functional unit to meet your business goals.

By acknowledging that every corporate family falls somewhere along a similar "Dysfunctional Continuum," where would you mark your company on the following scale?

> Problems are part of every family portrait, and no one is perfect.

22

Mild Dysfunction **>** *Moderate Dysfunction* **>** *Severe Dysfunction* **>** *Pathology*

LEADon has experienced companies all along the Dysfunctional Continuum over the years. Two of the worst scenarios we observed were in distinctly different kinds of corporate families. One happened to be a small, but unhealthy family-owned business; the other was a large, international corporation with a chaotic leadership team at its helm. In both situations, many employees were miserable despite the fiscal success of their respective businesses. While a few felt stuck in the pathological settings, others were leaving as quickly as they could find new corporate families in which they could fit.

> **There really is no "fun" in dysfunction.**

Although your company hopefully operates at the healthier end of this continuum, any dysfunction must be dealt with in order for you to create and develop the organizational dynasty you desire. Despite the old joke, there really is no "fun" in dysfunction. So, how can you as an exceptional leader assess, diagnose, and treat those troubling areas in your Corporate Family? You must begin by addressing family secrets, which often fall into one of five categories:

1. Roles and Responsibilities
2. Communication
3. Relational/Generational Conflicts
4. Conflict Resolution
5. Personal and Professional Life Balance

Let's look at the first category: Roles and Responsibilities. Many businesses have poorly defined roles and vague responsibilities that members on their organizational chart are supposed to follow. *The more unclear the expectations are for you and your coworkers, the more dysfunctional your company will be.* Specific boundaries allow fewer opportunities for family members to fail. For instance, you would never tell a teenager "Be home at a decent hour," but really expect him or her to be in before ten o'clock. Most of us realize (having been teenagers ourselves) that a pre-established deadline encourages a timely return. And if the time frame isn't met, there should be appropriate consequences. Clear expectations and follow-through are part of the process every family must implement in order to be successful.

> Specific boundaries allow fewer opportunities for family members to fail.

All corporate family members need clearly defined roles and responsibilities to ensure their success and the overall success of the business plan. High performance leaders must establish these guidelines, and they must enforce them, too. Sometimes this change to your corporate culture results in certain individuals becoming "free agents," and as much as their absence might cause temporary pain, the long-term health of the corporate family is what matters most.

> All corporate family members need clearly defined roles and responsibilities to ensure their success and the overall success of the business plan.

Communication is another category where secrets can abound. This problem is often seen in corporate gossip, with people spreading information about others. Whether through simple "chit-chat" or rumor-mill texting, these secrets can be harmful on many levels, especially to those corporate family members involved. We have seen corporate gossip divide teams and cripple business plans because of the grudges that typically follow. As a leader, you can set the best example by not being part of this form of detrimental communication and by encouraging employees to be careful about what they discuss and with whom they share important information.

Communication breakdowns are another area of concern. Some executives and employees use communication—or the lack thereof—as a means to control people. For example, one CEO we knew had a small cadre on the executive team who received constant communiqués about significant business matters. His CFO, however, was continually out of the loop. This intentional miscommunication on the CEO's part was his way of retaliating for a past offense that he was unwilling to forgive. You can only imagine the number of conflicts this created between the two executives and the rest of the leadership team.

> Some executives and employees use communication— or the lack thereof— as a means to control people.

Communication is a crucial area for exceptional leaders to focus and improve upon. Excellent communication involves "clarity," which means:

1. *No assumptions*
2. *No ambiguity*

If you think about how you communicate day in and day out, how often are you *truly clear* to those around you? Let's consider the typical Family of Procreation as an example. The husband says one thing, while the wife hears another. Parents give their children directives, but the kids thought something entirely different had been communicated. There are even times in these families when people wonder if a conversation ever took place!

The same types of miscommunication also occur routinely in all corporate families. Yet the more that you are able to communicate clearly—with no room for assumptions and no ambiguity—the better for everyone involved. And passing this vital skill to your Corporate Family members is just as critical. As everyone strives to be less ambiguous, opportunities for success increase. In addition, don't leave a meeting, finish a conversation, or send off an e-mail *assuming* someone understands what's been shared. Ask clarifying questions, and allow all team members to feel free to do the same.

> Yet the more that you are able to communicate clearly—with no room for assumptions and no ambiguity—the better for everyone involved.

The third area of family secrets involves Relational/Generational Conflicts. The aforementioned CEO was using a technique, called an "emotional triangle," with his CFO (the rest of the executive team represented the third part in this unhealthy triangle.) By pitting the CFO and the executive team against one another, the CEO had the power to manipulate both parties. Unfortunately, we see these emotional triangles in relationships and in many corporate settings. No one can be aligned and attuned when unity is in jeopardy, so leaders must discourage this form of family pathology at all costs. Playing "family favorites" can also be part of these dysfunctional triangles in corporate settings, and it leads to pain, frustration, and anger among employees. Your Corporate Family cannot afford unhealthy relationships if you hope to be

> Your Corporate Family cannot afford unhealthy relationships if you hope to be more productive and prosperous—not to mention eventually reach organizational dynasty status!

more productive and prosperous—not to mention eventually reach organizational dynasty status!

Strained relationships within and between generational groups can create difficulties in today's workplace. Although we will delve into this topic more deeply in Chapter 5, suffice it to say that your corporate setting is unlike any of previous decades because there are now four generations working together in many companies across America. The unique differences in your Corporate Family can create conflict, but they also provide great opportunity for improved productivity and profitability when leaders understand each generational group and utilize their respective skill sets for the benefit of the organization. How all of your employees relate and interact with one another will greatly impact your business, whether on the assembly line or the bottom line.

> Unique differences in your Corporate Family can create conflict, but they also provide great opportunity for improved productivity and profitability when leaders understand each generational group and utilize their respective skill sets for the benefit of the organization.

Another area of concern for the corporate family is Conflict Resolution. Few organizations have adequate practices in place to assist employees in dealing with the personal and interpersonal problems that are bound to arise throughout the workday. Yet, how many conflicts over the past days, weeks, months, and even years are part of the "secret" problems that you and your colleagues experience in your company? One organization LEADon assisted had a secretary in the main office who routinely conflicted with just about everyone. Although you might not think that one person out of fifty staff members could make too much of a negative impact, think again. This particular individual seemed to thrive on upsetting others, and sometimes this included clients. Even with intervention, the secretary refused to change. The best resolution for everyone in this instance was the "free agency" she was eventually given.

> There are many positive principles that can be readily implemented to help resolve conflict in your business.

There are many positive principles that can be readily implemented to help resolve conflict in your business. At LEADon, we encourage leaders and their High Performance Teams to integrate a twelve-step process of conflict resolution into their corporate culture. Exceptional leaders must help their corporate families learn to resolve conflict. You need to establish a plan based on shared values that every employee is willing to accept, implement, and be accountable to it. The sooner you help your Corporate Family members learn to resolve conflict, the happier and healthier your work environment will become.

In *The Leading Edge: 9 Strategies for Improving Internal and Intentional Leadership* (Wilke & Wilke, 2010), we discuss an area of weakness for many executives and their employees:

> When our personal lives are out of balance, it negatively impacts us professionally—and vice versa.

the lack of Personal and Professional Life Balance. Dysfunction in this vital area creates all kinds of problems for people in today's workforce. When our personal lives are out of balance, it negatively impacts us professionally—and vice versa. Any number of problems can affect this balance, from relationships gone awry, to chemical dependency, to financial struggles, to loneliness and isolation. Companies suffer when corporate family members don't take proper care of themselves and fail to keep all aspects of their lives in balance.

This area is extremely important for you as a leader to assess, diagnose, and treat, first in your own life and then in your Corporate Family members. If your life is in disarray, you'll never be a true role model for others! And, if you allow colleagues to continue down a negative path without intervention, you could be allowing that dysfunction to progress toward pathology.

The five categories of potential family secrets are essential to acknowledge. Although this is a difficult process for most of us, exceptional leaders must confront any and all dysfunctional elements impacting their corporate families. Part of your role and responsibilities is to address these "secrets" in your own Corporate Family closet—beginning with you first, then the rest of the family.

We'd like to conclude this topic by sharing a story about a corporate family secret we encountered several years ago. It happened to involve pornography—an area of concern for many families, including corporate families. In this case, an international public company established a policy of "zero tolerance" for pornography, which was backed by both the legal and human resource departments. In other words, if porn was found on any company computer, it was cause for immediate termination.

> Part of your role and responsibilities is to address these "secrets" in your own Corporate Family closet—beginning with you first, then the rest of the family.

Several months after this policy was established, a senior vice president's computer was serviced. It was riddled with pornographic sites, and he was promptly fired. Within thirty days, the new COO also had a problem with porn sites on his computer at work. Because he was a hot commodity for the corporation (and a relative of one of the owners), this "family favorite" retained his job despite the zero tolerance policy.

Many corporate family members were outraged by the double standard, lack of accountability, and favoritism by those in leadership—but this situation disappeared into the corporate family closet, so it has become one of this company's bitter secrets.

Although you are probably aware of many of your company's secrets, now is the time to properly assess, diagnose, and treat them before you and your business move any farther along the Dysfunctional Continuum toward pathology.

Many leaders require assistance with this process, much like real family members who seek out a counselor or psychologist to help resolve their personal dilemmas. The reason for this aid is simple: objective professionals can usually identify problems much easier than those within the family unit. So, seek guidance as needed. Don't be afraid to ask your Corporate Family members for feedback and insights. Look to your mentors and other trustworthy people in your sphere of influence for advice about improvement and how best to achieve these critical changes. Most importantly, start by taking an honest look at the secrets your Corporate Family may be hiding. When you do, you'll be fulfilling your own leadership role and responsibilities as "parent" to your Corporate Family members.

FAMILY TIME

1. What kinds of "secrets" have you had to deal with in your personal and professional families? Write them down.

2. List specific Corporate Family secrets that need to be addressed by you and your High Performance Team. Force rank and prioritize these in order of importance.

3. Provide some solutions to each of the barriers to greatness you listed in question #2. How can you appropriately share these solutions with all members of your Corporate Family?

Meet the Parents

*Children begin by loving their parents; as they grow older
they judge them; sometimes they forgive them.*

Oscar Wilde, The Picture of Dorian Gray

Jim Chandler never thought his role as President and COO
would include the responsibility of parenting. In fact, his
dream of operating his own business stemmed more from his
passion for the product rather than the need to lead people.
But lead people he did—more than three hundred and fifty of
them worked at his plant located in an industrial area of a large
metropolitan city.

These people, Jim's "corporate family," required his attention on a regular basis. Jim was surprised by how much of his
day was consumed with people problems. Sometimes there
were disputes among his executive team that required his
intervention. More often than seemed necessary, members of

the management team wanted his input and ideas. Even his assistant had been experiencing numerous personal problems lately, and she performed her tasks better if he took time to check in with her and listen to the latest crisis.

Lauren Ramirez usually enjoyed feeling like a parent to the group of mostly Millennial generation members in her employ. She ran a small chain of coffee stores that she and her father had started eight years prior. Young people liked working in the chic environment she'd created, and Lauren tried to accommodate their varying schedules, mostly dictated by the courses they took at school. Yet Lauren had begun to grow weary of the demands some of these younger employees put upon her, and she was tired of being taken for granted as she tried to adjust work schedules. Lately she'd had to put in a lot of extra hours in order to cover for absentee employees. Plus Lauren also spent countless hours counseling some of these employees through their personal problems, which caused her own work to pile up and increased her stress level.

> **Parents, by definition, are the leaders within a family.**

Do Jim and Lauren's dilemmas sound familiar? Welcome to the world of corporate parenting. Although you've never seen this responsibility listed in any employee contract you've signed and more than likely it was never discussed in any of your business courses or internship programs, parenting is part of every leader's ultimate responsibilities. *Parents, by definition, are the leaders within a family.* In our personal lives, the parenting role is quite obvious: when people have children, they become parents—and with that role comes corresponding responsibilities. This is equally true in our corporate families, though a little less obvious: when you become the leader of men and women in your organization, parenting will be part of the process.

So, if you're an executive or part of a leadership team, you are looked up to just like parents are in any family setting. If you happen to be a leader on the management team, then those under you expect "parental" guidance from you. Even if you lead a small team of people, your role and responsibilities include "parenting" those men and women within your sphere of influence.

> The most productive families—and those that leave a lasting legacy—succeed because of the intentional efforts of the parents.

The most productive families—and those that leave a lasting legacy—succeed because of the intentional efforts of the parents. How they "do" family makes all of the difference. If parents are weak and ineffective, the family suffers. However, if parents are strong, involved, positive, and proactive, the family has a tremendous chance of not only surviving but also thriving!

> If parents are strong, involved, positive, and proactive, the family has a tremendous chance of not only surviving but also thriving!

Part of good parenting includes creating an environment that is conducive for each family member's success. In the corporate world, we call this environment the "culture." Companies with strong corporate cultures tend to be more productive and profitable, and they are the ones that often achieve organizational dynasty status. They develop and maintain a place of business where everyone involved feels good about being there and great about what they're doing. In other words, the culture the

> The culture the parents create provides opportunities for success.

parents create provides opportunities for success. (We will cover much more on culture in Chapter 8, and *The Leading Edge* also details how to improve your corporate culture).

As part of cultural development, leaders/parents have three fundamental responsibilities to those in their care. They must:

1. Set standards,
2. Role-model these standards, and
3. Encourage accountability for all Corporate Family members as they embrace these standards.

Setting standards includes establishing guidelines for how business is to be conducted in your organization. It means clearly defining business goals and objectives, as well as detailing specific roles and responsibilities for everyone on the organizational chart. In addition, leaders must determine whether or not the corporate family will be run in a flat or bureaucratic manner.

> Leaders must determine whether or not the corporate family will be run in a flat or bureaucratic manner.

Bureaucratic organizations tend to be strict and rigid. The culture of these businesses is built upon numerous rules, procedures, policies, and manuals. Some businesses operate best in a bureaucratic fashion. Law enforcement, government, the military, and energy providers (e.g., electrical and nuclear power plants) are some examples where a bureaucratic culture produces the best results.

On the other hand, flat organizations operate more freely than bureaucratic ones. These organizations are principle-based and rely heavily on personal responsibility to the virtues and values of the corporate family culture. Executives hold the power, but family members participate in setting the culture and are encouraged to fulfill their roles and responsibilities on a level playing field. "Flat" describes the way all employees conduct themselves so they can work together to meet the objectives of the business plan. In other words, because of flexibility and an environment that is less rigid, corporate family members are encouraged to be creative, innovative, and entrepreneurial. *But take note: just because a business is flat doesn't mean everyone is equal.* Instead, everyone is expected to participate in an open, transparent manner as they fulfill their *respective* roles and responsibilities.

> Flat organizations also often meet the diverse generational needs of the current workforce.

At LEADon, we urge leaders to evaluate whether their organization should be run in a flat or bureaucratic manner. We believe that flat systems are better for most professional settings. Flat organizations also often meet the diverse generational needs of the current workforce (we'll discuss this further in Chapter 5), and they increase the potential for innovation, creativity, and group genius. These businesses usually exceed business plans and goals.

Yet there are also instances when even flat organizations must become more bureaucratic for the good of the corporate family. In times of economic downturn, leaders may need to establish stricter guidelines and controls in order to survive in a difficult market. This more stringent structure provides safety and security for everyone involved in the day-to-day operations. When the crisis has passed, a flatter system can resume.

> The bottom line is that leaders are ultimately responsible for determining how flat or bureaucratic their company can and should be.

The bottom line is that leaders are ultimately responsible for determining how flat or bureaucratic their company

> Your employees will be looking up to you and your executive team as children look to their parents.

can and should be. The establishment of this fundamental standard of business will guide employees as they meet other benchmarks. And all standards for your business must be role-modeled by you, the exceptional leader. This is a responsibility that you cannot abdicate. Your employees will be looking up to you and your executive team as children look to their parents. What kids see, they put into practice. For instance, if a mom says "Don't lie Annie; it's not right," but then is observed lying about Annie's age to get her into the movies at a cheaper rate, what is the girl more likely to follow—the words or the actions?

> Actions always win out over words!

Actions always win out over words! While some men and women express, "Do as I say, not as I do," human nature leans toward the reverse of this axiom. *Leaders must lead; there can be no exceptions.* Besides, if words were enough to keep your Corporate Family members in check, most days you could simply stay home in your pajamas! The problem is that people require positive role-modeling and accountability on a regular, consistent basis in order to be successful.

> Leaders must lead; there can be no exceptions.

Another key to the success of any principle-based culture is the concept of mutual accountability. In other words, all members of the corporate family should be expected to hold one another accountable to the culture and standards they've agreed upon. The accountability must be consistent with everyone on the organizational chart, from

> Another key to the success of any principle-based culture is the concept of mutual accountability.

the CEO to the receptionist. You are your brother's and sister's keeper! If someone isn't fulfilling his or her role or responsibilities, the situation will be addressed directly with the individual in a respectful manner. Accountability isn't about confrontation. We prefer a direct conversation that specifies where the standards have not been met and how this scenario must be improved in the immediate future. Directness is always preferred to confrontation.

> **Directness is always preferred to confrontation.**

While mutual accountability includes your participation, as an exceptional leader you must also realize that your investment in the Corporate Family comes with higher risks. Parents are ultimately responsible for the actions of their children. This is what we meant earlier when we said everyone is not totally equal in your organization, even if you choose to operate in a flat system. When push comes to shove, the leader/parent is responsible for the goals and objectives being achieved. *Results are the primary objective in any corporate family!* Moreover, children/corporate family members typically do not go to jail when certain standards are violated, though parents/executives can. Therefore, you must take this parental role seriously and actively engage in it for your own good and the benefit of your company.

> **Results are the primary objective in any corporate family!**

> **Great parents are usually easy to spot.**

Great parents are usually easy to spot. They care for their children and provide for their needs. They set up healthy boundaries, hold their progeny accountable to standards, and follow-through with consequences for inappropriate behavior.

> They praise, practice what they preach, and always take time to play!

They praise, practice what they preach, and always take time to play!

As for bad parents…well, you can probably think of an example from your professional life. Take a few minutes to reflect on your years in the workforce. Did you ever have a boss that was a bad "parent" to you and your co-workers? What experiences come to mind when you think of this leader?

When we ask our clients to share from their professional history, the list of examples goes on and on. For many, negative experiences inspired them to strive to do things differently in their own corporate families. This is also why so many of these leaders incorporate internal and intentional leadership development within their corporate family settings.

> The job of parenting is a tough one no matter what your family looks like.

Some of the good "parents" we've met include people like Jim Chandler and Lauren Ramirez. While they struggled with some of their responsibilities as leaders/parents in their respective corporate families, they realized that, in order to be most productive and profitable, they needed to fully embrace their roles. They required some "counseling" (i.e., leadership development) to improve their skill sets and help the rest of their corporate family members learn how to better fulfill their own roles and responsibilities. They also wanted additional guidance on how they could lead their companies to even greater success.

Parents need this type of extra support from time to time, even if they've been doing great. The job of parenting is a tough one no matter what your family looks like. And in order to build lasting dynasties that leave a positive legacy, parents also need to have fun with their families. This piece of the parenting puzzle doesn't always compute in the corporate world. Some leaders say, "Fun? How can we have fun when we're struggling to increase productivity?"

While it may seem counterintuitive, having fun together makes your Corporate Family a more cohesive team. Times of celebration are part of the Behavior Patterns that your colleagues and coworkers need to spur one another on to even greater successes. So, take time to plan and initiate Corporate Family gatherings. Whether these are informal "happy hour" events or organized parties, get everyone on your organizational chart together on a regular, consistent basis. Integrate rapport building activities into your meetings, especially ones that support your Values, Beliefs, and Behavior Patterns (we'll delve deeper into the topic of celebrating in Chapter 10).

> While it may seem counterintuitive, having fun together makes your Corporate Family a more cohesive team.

> Good parents are invested in raising up the next generation of leadership.

Finally, good parents are invested in raising up the next generation of leadership. These parents realize that they won't be around forever and that leaving a lasting legacy must include preparing second-level leaders in their succession plan. Parents must prepare and equip future leaders with the skill sets necessary to assume their own executive/parenting roles down the road.

Parents in any family lead in one manner or another, so it's your decision how you will approach this critical role in your Corporate Family. By developing a great culture and intentionally working on standards, role-modeling, and accountability, you will be well on your way to leaving an incredible legacy. And you will also become the kind of parent that any Corporate Family member would be proud to emulate.

FAMILY TIME

1. Who are the parents in your Corporate Family?

2. Who in your Corporate Family seems best prepared for their parenting/executive role? Why?

3. How is your Corporate Family performing as it pertains to accountability?

4. Is your business more bureaucratic or flat in its operations?

5. Who in your next level of leadership is best suited to become an outstanding executive/ parent someday? What steps are you taking to develop their leadership skill sets?

Chapter FOUR

Siblings—
and Their Rivalry

*...the accursed rivalry which brought sister nations and
brother people to fight one another. I do not feel happy for this
victory of mine. On the contrary, I would be glad, brothers, if
I had all of you standing here next to me, since we are united
by the same language, the same blood and the same visions.*

Alexander the Great, Historiae Alexandri Magni

In any family, whether personal or professional, sibling rivalry
does and always will exist. Because of this reality, it's the
responsibility of parents to minimize conflicts and teach the
crucial life skills of conflict resolution and unity. Depending
upon experiences in your Family of Origin and Family of
Procreation (see Chapter 1), your ability to address problems
that arise among the "children" in your Corporate Family may
be limited. This chapter will offer specific strategies on how to
solve these relational issues so that you and all family members
in your organization can operate at an optimum level.

Interestingly, sibling rivalry can occur at *all levels* of the
corporate family. This means that the "parents" (the leaders in

> Sibling rivalry can occur at all levels of the corporate family.

the organization) can experience the same types of power, control, and conflict issues as the "children" (all other employees) in a company. This is because sibling rivalry, at its very essence, is about competition between brothers and sisters—whether blood-related or corporately united. And while we know that healthy competition can enhance creativity and productivity,

> Sibling rivalry, at its very essence, is about competition between brothers and sisters—whether blood-related or corporately united.

unhealthy competiveness can be divisive and destructive. The latter is why balance is so important in family life—including the interactions between all members of your Corporate Family.

Rivalry between siblings is natural because this is one way that people individuate; each of us attempts to define who we are as individuals even though we are part of a larger group. In addition, children often strive to get their parents' attention, especially if they feel they aren't being noticed or responded to appropriately. Also, without training in how to resolve conflict—well, kids will be kids. They will fuss, argue, and even fight with one another until proper boundaries have been put in place and they learn more productive ways of dealing with the daily problems that arise.

Within the corporate family, the causes of most sibling rivalry can be classified into the following two categories:

1. Power and Control Issues (dominance)
2. Unresolved Conflict (including gossip and grudges)

Struggling for power and control is part of being human. All of us attempt to have a sense of control over our environment to one degree or another. Some men and women have a higher need for control than others, and usually these are the kinds of people who seek leadership positions. With leadership comes power, another driving force in human achievement. However, the balance point between power and control in our lives and in how we interact with others (who have their own power/control issues) is often where we experience trouble.

> In corporate life, power and control struggles between individuals and groups can cause isolation and fragmentation.

In corporate life, power and control struggles between individuals and groups can cause isolation and fragmentation. When people become isolated, we call this phenomenon the *"silo effect;"* at this point, the alignment and attunement of your Corporate Family will be in jeopardy.

The silo effect is a term taken from farming and agriculture. If individuals and/or teams feel like they are off on their own, operating as if they were located in some silo with little or no connection to the rest of the corporate family, then a sense of distance and fragmentation sets in. These isolated men and women even-

> These isolated men and women eventually become disinterested in and disengaged from the overall needs of the organization.

tually become disinterested in and disengaged from the overall needs of the organization. As they pull away, unity and cohesion in your Corporate Family become harder and harder to maintain. So, while some people gain power, others feel separated from the corporate family.

At LEADon, we've seen this scenario far too often in businesses. It doesn't matter the type of industry or the size of the company, unbridled power and control issues wreak havoc on productivity and profitability. In a service organization we worked with many years ago, the operational and field departments constantly strove to undermine one another, in part to prove how important their particular "high performing" team was and to gain the attention of leadership. The result was complete chaos and an increasing number of incidents of outward conflict. These two groups in the same corporate family were quickly moving from a family feud to outright civil war.

When the team at LEADon met with these two departments separately, we discovered a common theme to their power/control issues: neither group thought the other understood or appreciated what they did on a daily basis. The field team felt used, abused, and disrespected by the organizational staff. These men and women also expressed dissatisfaction for operational decision-making that didn't include their input. Similarly, the operational department shared that they sensed a lack of appreciation from the field workers for their roles and responsibilities, including all they did to help the team members in meeting goals and objectives.

The good news for this organization is that they identified this escalating problem before it culminated in a major corporate crisis. Over time, we were able to assist in improving communication between groups. Monthly meetings were established in which these family members could talk about issues and strategize together about how to resolve problems. In addition, quarterly gatherings were initiated by leadership so that all members of the corporate family could build rapport, improve relationships, and celebrate successes. The leaders of the company also took an active role by learning new skills sets and developing habits to improve their own "parenting" abilities. Soon they were cascading these essential life skills to all levels of the organization.

Power and control issues play an interesting role during transitional times within companies. For instance, when new leadership takes over, employees frequently feel insecure about their current and future job status. Any shift in power can make individuals sense that things are out-of-control, and this can lead to "acting out" among family members. While we'll discuss more specifics about transitions in Chapter 6, it's vital that you recognize how aspects of power and control impact the interactions of your Corporate Family.

> Any shift in power can make individuals sense that things are out-of-control, and this can lead to "acting out" among family members.

As we mentioned earlier, competition is a normal aspect of being a sibling, no matter what setting you find yourself in. History is replete with healthy and unhealthy examples of sibling rivalry. Think of the ancient stories of Cain and Abel, Rachel and Leah, or Joseph and his eleven brothers. In his quote at the beginning of this chapter, Alexander the Great grieved as he gazed upon the dead soldiers strewn across a battlefield—who he considered to be like lost brothers. Shakespeare wrote numerous plays based on siblings and their rivalries. Remember King Lear's son, Edmund, who forced his half-brother into exile, or the two sisters, Kate and Bianca, in *The Taming of the Shrew*? There are more contemporary (and healthier) examples of competing siblings, such as Peyton and Eli Manning of American football fame, or Venus and Serena Williams in the world of tennis.

Those children who are encouraged to express themselves in a balance of cooperation and competition become successful, and the family unit grows healthier. This success leads to the second cause of most sibling rivalry that parents must deal with: unresolved conflict. Like competition, open conflict is

> There will never be a conflict free zone in any family unit, especially in your Corporate Family.

guaranteed when two or more are gathered together. There will never be a conflict free zone in any family unit, especially in your Corporate Family. With all of the different people in your organization from various backgrounds, cultures, and experiences, there will always be a wide array of ideas, opinions, and ways of doing things. So when the inevitable conflicts do occur, the most successful teams are those that properly and positively address those issues.

> A clearly defined system for resolving conflict is the best solution to these scenarios.

A clearly defined system for resolving conflict is the best solution to these scenarios. This requires devising a conflict resolution plan that all members of your Corporate Family help construct and commit themselves to, no matter what. At LEADon, we train leaders in a 12-Step Conflict Resolution process that works in any company setting. Once your Corporate Family becomes aligned and attuned to your plan for conflict resolution, there must also be accountability among and between individuals and teams. In other words, everyone is to abide by the established rules for how your organization will deal with conflict, and if these steps are violated, members of your Corporate Family will quickly and specifically address the problem with respective consequences as part of the agreed accountability.

> Once your Corporate Family becomes aligned and attuned to your plan for conflict resolution, there must also be accountability among and between individuals and teams.

How the parents lead this conflict resolution process is critical. As it should be in our personal families, the parenting role involves teaching children how to resolve conflict. Parents cannot do this merely with words; they also must role-model these skill sets on a daily basis. Unfortunately a common weakness among leaders is the temptation to shy away from circumstances that include conflict. We've heard a variety of excuses for this, including:

> How the parents lead this conflict resolution process is critical.

1. "I'm not involved in that issue, so they should work it out on their own."
2. "They're getting paid, so it's their job to get things back on track."
3. "They better work it out because if it continues, I'll fire them!"

The last statement was shared with us not long ago by a CEO, and he was quite serious.

His method of dealing with conflict involved a "hands off" policy until the chaos bothered him too much—then he simply fired people. Talk about a waste of valuable resources and talent! Would anyone ever dream that would yield positive results? Imagine what would happen in any Family of Procreation when children became too obnoxious or bickered incessantly, so parents decided to give them free agency. We'd have a society of homeless children, childless "families," and a completely chaotic society!

> As difficult as it may be, leaders need to equip their employees on how to address conflict appropriately.

As difficult as it may be, leaders need to equip their employees on how to address conflict appropriately. They must establish the "rules of engagement" for healthy debating versus destructive

> Sadly, we've seen such conflicts turn viral—sometimes crossing time zones and continents in international corporations before the end of a single business day.

disputing. Kids simply don't know how to "work things out" on their own, so how can we expect fifty to five thousand people to get together in our Corporate Family settings and interact appropriately without some sort of guidance? Without clear expectations for these family members, you will have fifty to five thousand styles of conflict resolution in constant operation— a situation that can only negatively impact your Profit and Loss statement. Instead of the unity you desire, you'll soon have a Corporate Family civil war brewing. Sadly, we've seen such conflicts turn viral—sometimes crossing time zones and continents in international corporations before the end of a single business day.

The solutions to sibling rivalry can be summarized fairly succinctly:

1. Leaders must be intentional in their coaching and mentoring of individuals and teams, preparing and equipping them to balance power and control and appropriately address conflict.
2. Power struggles must be minimized within the Corporate Family. Leaders do this by role-modeling unity, empowering family members, and encouraging teamwork.
3. Leaders must become experts in conflict resolution and learn how to "Eustress."

> Power struggles must be minimized within the Corporate Family.

Eustress is an interesting concept that involves finding a healthy, integrated balance between stress and distress. In *The*

Leading Edge, we explain that leaders must strive for this balance if they hope to be successful over time. Eustress is also an essential life skill to cascade to your colleagues and co-workers alike, because stress in parents' and children's lives only fuels the fire to further conflict and sibling rivalry.

A beautiful example of what happens when a company learns how to deal with sibling rivalry can be found in Orange County, California. Disney's California Adventure Park has been undergoing a complete makeover, and in 2010, an amazing new attraction, called *World of Color,* was unveiled. The twenty-five-minute show took five years to plan, program, and construct, and it includes a continuous water screen that covers nineteen thousand square feet and hovers fifty feet high. Yet his man-made marvel would never have been completed without a leadership team that was able to effectively bring all of the "kids" in this corporate family together.

Usually Disney animators, Pixar animators, and Imagineers work independently on their various ventures, especially after some difficult family history over the past few decades. For this particular project, however, the "parents" decided to try something different. The result is an amalgamation of creativity, talent, and teamwork. Instead of distinct groups—perhaps even "siloed" departments—the siblings were able to work cooperatively toward a common goal. And, based on the overwhelming response of their clientele, they completely surpassed expectations.

That's our goal for you too. We'd like nothing better than for you to attain this kind of synergy in your company so that the only thing you can say about the siblings is how great they get along. By intentionally addressing the aspects of rivalry within your Corporate Family, you can deal with any unhealthy habits and move to a position of peace and harmony as well as increased productivity and profitability. As you grow and develop in these critical areas of leadership, you'll be competent to help your Corporate Family prepare for future successes in the organizational dynasty you're creating and developing.

FAMILY TIME

1. Identify both the "public" and "secret" rivalries in your Corporate Family. Write them down.

2. Consider how these rivalries impact your business plan. Label each as either *productive* or *destructive*.

3. Does your Corporate Family embrace and practice a clear, effective method for resolving conflict? If not, what steps can you take to develop a conflict resolution plan?

4. How can you and your leadership team begin to improve negative sibling rivalry in your Corporate Family? What types of accountability measures would help individuals and teams in this process?

Chapter FIVE

Generations and Gender Working Together

The great cycle of the ages is renewed. Now Justice returns, returns the Golden Age; a new generation now descends from on high.

Virgil, Eclogues

Warning: The topics in this chapter tend to spark strong reactions from both men and women. In our experiences with some clients, we've seen men roll their eyes, whisper to each other, pull out their Blackberries, or blow us off altogether. In certain groups, women have become upset, defensive, teary, or angry. Some people are uncomfortable discussing issues related to age and/or gender, so we're asking you to lower your defenses, open yourself to new insights, and embrace those differences that make our corporate families unique!

Joe Davis looked over his reading glasses at the co-workers he'd assembled. The three were reviewing the report he'd prepared with varying degrees of enthusiasm. Michele Suzuki-Hines, one of his C-level executives, was highlighting a section of the document. Nate Shulman was opening his laptop with one hand and thumbing through the report with the other. Kiesha Williams appeared to be skimming over the cover page as she typed some sort of message on her iPhone.

"At this rate, I'll never be able to retire," Joe thought to himself. *"Look at these future leaders of my company! Michele might run things okay, but I'm not sure she can handle the others who look like they could care less!"* As if she could hear his thoughts, Michele looked up from the report.

"Joe, this appears to be a lot of important material to cover this late on a Friday. I think we need to get together tomorrow morning to make sure we're all on the same page," Michele stated frankly.

"Tomorrow!" Nate spouted, a shocked expression on his face. "I can't be here then. My kids have games on Saturday and Sunday, and I'm not going to miss those."

"Yeah," Kiesha added, glancing up nonchalantly from her iPhone. "I agree with Nate. I can't give up my weekends." She immediately went back to the message she was texting.

———

While you're reading this book, scenes like this are being played out in companies all across America. In fact, they may be happening in your Corporate Family right now. Teams of all sizes experience differences in how they think, process, plan, and work together, and many of the distinctions are due to generational and gender differences.

> There are currently four generational groups interacting in today's workplace.

As we discuss at length in *The Leading Edge,* there are currently four generational groups interacting in today's workplace. These groups include the Silent Generation,

Baby Boomers, Gen Xers, and Millennials. Each generation has been defined by cultural and societal influences, and members of these generational cohorts think and behave in unique ways because of those forces. Everything from parenting styles to technological advances impact how people act both at home and at work, and exceptional leaders must be aware of how these differences impact the experiences within their corporate families.

From the story above, Joe Davis is a prime example of someone from the Silent Generation (those born between 1924 and 1945). He helped build the company he now runs, and he is determined to keep what he'd worked so hard for strong and successful. This drive to strengthen what has been built is why men and women from the Silent Generation are often labeled "Builders." After the events of the Great Depression and World War II, members of this group aided in rebuilding America along with their predecessors, the Greatest Generation. Although many of them have retired in recent years, others have not done so due to their intense work ethic. Like Joe, members of this generation struggle to understand the mindset of younger employees who don't seem to share the same enthusiasm for their business and its overall goals and objectives.

> This drive to strengthen what has been built is why men and women from the Silent Generation are often labeled "Builders."

Michele Suzuki-Hines is an excellent representative of Baby Boomers (anyone born between 1946 and 1964). Before Joe called the meeting to order, she'd begun scanning the report he'd given. Already in action, Michele was also more than willing to work the whole weekend if necessary to get the new plan going. Members of the Baby Boom Generation were strongly impacted by the Silent Generation's work ethic, and because of their surprisingly explosive population (thus the "boom" descriptor), these Boomers felt that they were called to change their world. Indeed, their revolutionary ideas helped reshape the culture of the United States, including providing more opportunities for women and minorities in the workforce.

> Boomers felt that they were called to change their world.

Nate Shulman's shock at being asked to work on weekends reveals Gen Xers' (those born between 1965 and 1980) tendency to value the joys of living over their professional calling. After being raised by high-achieving Baby Boomers, members of Generation X rebelled against the push to succeed while risking quality of life and relationships. Part of this rebellion sprang from the fact that, as children, members of Generation X were often latch key kids while parents worked. Also, they experienced the increased divorce rate, leaving many in single parent homes or in newly formed stepfamilies. While these societal changes made Gen Xers strongly independent, as adults they have embraced the need for family and "a life" over financial or positional gain.

> Generation X rebelled against the push to succeed while risking quality of life and relationships.

The enthusiasm for technology and multitasking define Kiesha William's Millennial Generation (anyone born between 1981 and 2000) perfectly. The youngest members of our corporate families have been raised by parents, teachers, and communities who protected and praised them as a "special" group. Because of this insulation and the economic surplus during their youth, Millennials are also accustomed to instant rewards and gratification. They welcome diversity, and they've never known a world without technology. In fact, Millennials' simultaneous utilization of multiple technologies can create conflict with senior team members, and their constant need to interact with others, manifested in texting and "tweeting," is often misinterpreted as disinterest in work-related matters.

> Millennials' simultaneous utilization of multiple technologies can create conflict with senior team members.

Interestingly, these generational differences happen in every family, including our Corporate Families. Whether in our personal homes or our "home away from home," grandparents, parents, and kids experience conflict due to the differences in the age groups. The younger generation often feels the older one is "out of touch" with what's going on.

Senior members of the family say things like "What's wrong with those kids?" or "When I was their age, I never would have done something like that!" The problem is that this cynical cycle doesn't get us anywhere! *Every generation has been, is, and will be unique.* The only way to bring everyone together is to begin to understand these generational differences, embrace them, and, yes, even celebrate them.

> Every generation has been, is, and will be unique.

As a leader, navigating generational waters requires that you become a Cultural Translator. First, you must understand the characteristics and nuances of each generational group in your employ. Next, you need to equip all leaders and staff with skills so they can appreciate these differences and build upon one another's strengths. Finally, you should actively intercede and "translate" among these cultural groups to ensure clear communication and operations within your organization.

> As a leader, navigating generational waters requires that you become a Cultural Translator.

There are many books available that can help you increase your knowledge of these generational groups; we've listed a few in the *Recommended Reading* section for you. However, you may find that you and your leaders need to spend more time learning skill sets to improve the relationships between Corporate Family members. This is where specific leadership development training may be of tremendous assistance to you and your organization.

> All men are not the same. All women are not the same. And certainly men and women are not the same.

Similar dynamics are at play in relation to gender differences in the workplace. While we agree with the Declaration of Independence's statement that we are all created equal, it does not mean that we are all the same, nor does it guarantee equal results. There are differences within and between genders—wonderful, inspiring, awesome differences!

All men are not the same. All women are not the same. And certainly men and women are not the same. Can you imagine what a bland and boring world we would live in if we were?

Some time ago we were asked to facilitate a corporate event that included men and women from several regional offices. The one hundred and twenty-five team members who'd been assembled by eight executive leaders stayed actively engaged in the various communication skill-building activities that we incorporated throughout the day-long meeting. However, during the feedback session with the executive team afterwards, several of the men were upset that we had brought up gender issues. They stated frankly that they were tired of women complaining about things in their company. Then two of the female executives spoke up; they fumed that the men even noticed anything about gender during the meeting. In their opinion, everyone should be the same in the company.

For the first time that day, we were speechless. Had we all attended the same meeting? Communication had been the theme, and that's what all of the LEADon materials had covered. But these organizers of the session had become so wrapped around the issue of gender that they'd missed the powerful impact the workshop had on the rest of their team. And rather than accepting the reality that had been in front of them all day—the presence and influence of men and women from all kinds of backgrounds, cultures, and experiences—they were arguing about something completely unachievable: *sameness.*

It is our uniqueness that allows for a rich array of ideas, insights, and creativity. In addition to physiological differences, there are philosophical and pragmatic distinctions in how males and females approach life and work. Every family, whether personal or professional, must learn to respect this *most elemental aspect* of diversity for the overall health, happiness, and success of everyone involved.

> Every family, whether personal or professional, must learn to respect this *most elemental aspect* of diversity for the overall health, happiness, and success of everyone involved.

For instance, consider what happens in a family when the father constantly speaks disrespectfully to the mother. What kind of example is set when a mom regularly chastises a dad in front of the kids? Would you ever allow your sons to battle and brawl over issues or let your daughters carry on screaming matches with one another? Imagine the constant conflict such families would be in! And what on earth would the next generation look like with these kinds of role models?

Our corporate families should strive for understanding and acceptance within and between genders. The "parents" (leadership) must role-model the importance of gender as well as generational differences as the "children" (the rest of the staff) are watching them. *Remember leaders: actions speak louder than words.* So, just because you establish a corporate policy against sexual harassment doesn't mean your work has been completed. You must follow that policy yourself, and there should also be corporate-wide accountability. If you state that your organization is going to respect generational differences, but then you say something about "those lazy interns" during a meeting, you're undermining your role as Cultural Translator.

> **Remember leaders: actions speak louder than words.**

We've seen tremendous growth in companies as leaders have embraced these insights and striven to become Cultural Translators within their organizations. Perhaps one of the most exciting transformations we've observed has been in the construction management industry. During the past few decades, more and more women have not only become part of the profession, but they have also moved into leadership positions at an unprecedented rate. While they've had to overcome many firmly entrenched barriers and "old school" mentalities, these women have added fresh perspectives and are forging a leadership path for younger generations of females to follow.

Similar success stories are occurring in numerous organizations across the country where leaders have recognized problems between generations and have striven to address those dilemmas directly. Older, not-so-old, and younger team members can work well together despite the natural differences that exist because of the influences of their specific generational groups. The senior members in the business help uphold the values and traditions of the company, while younger team members bring innovative ideas and openness to advances in their respective industries.

And any weakness their specific backgrounds may bring is often compensated for by the strengths of those from different generational and gender groups.

> Any weakness their specific backgrounds may bring is often compensated for by the strengths of those from different generational and gender groups.

Take an inventory of your Corporate Family today. Which generational groups exist in your workforce? If you're in a large company, there may be many members from all four generational groups we've discussed. If your business is smaller, the generational influences may seem simpler, but they are real nonetheless! How about gender issues? Do you see the differences in and between the genders, or are you trying to treat everyone exactly the same? If so, perhaps this inaccurate perception is why the men and women on your team seem tense, unhappy, or distant. If they can't be who they truly are at work, how can you expect them to be productive?

Every family across the globe deals with generational and gender concerns. If you hope to achieve the goals and objectives of your business plan, then you must encourage your Corporate Family members to understand, embrace, and celebrate these differences so that everyone can effectively work together. When you do, your organization will definitely be on the path toward greatness—and so will you!

FAMILY TIME

1. How many "generations" exist in your Corporate Family? Name/identify them.

2. Have a meal with all generations present. Read this chapter and discuss the generational characteristics with each specific group.

3. Do you think the genders are the same? Should they be the same? Should we accommodate any differences? If so, how?

4. Can you list any specific generational or gender problems in your Corporate Family? What solutions would you recommend to improve these situations?

Divorce, Remarriage, and Blended Corporate Families

Marriage is about love; divorce is about money.

Anonymous

Throughout the years, LEADon has worked with many types of companies. Some have been true family businesses, owned and operated by generations of genetically-linked men and women. Other organizations have been joined together by commonality of purpose and creative ideas and ideals. These corporate marriages have ranged from small to large businesses, public and private, for-profit and non-profit. Yet all of these unique families have similar characteristics: *their passion and commitment to their partnership.*

In some cases, these unions have been composed of happy, healthy corporate family members who functioned well together and achieved varying degrees of success. These corporate marriages have been productive and profitable in their respective industries, and some of them are on their way to attaining "organizational dynasty" status. But we've also worked with other firms that were struggling, sometimes on the verge of a full-blown corporate divorce. After all, the challenges of business can impact the best relationships. Sometimes communication had broken down, and no one knew how to rebuild a united team. For a few companies, neglect over time resulted in differences and distance between people, and unresolved conflicts that once appeared trivial suddenly seemed cataclysmic.

Recently, we heard the story of three psychiatrists who formed a company because of their shared philosophies and passion for helping people. They purchased an old building and remodeled it for their thriving practice. Yet, over the course of several years, circumstances changed. These friends and colleagues started feuding over small issues, and before long, they dissolved their practice, putting their renovated building on the market in a "fire sale." What happened to cause such a major rift between former friends? If three *psychiatrists* experienced such severe problems in keeping their "marriage" together, how will the rest of us be able to maintain unity in our corporate families?

> As a leader, you must internally and intentionally strive to achieve the goals of your business plan while simultaneously developing the men and women who comprise your Corporate Family in order to maintain a productive and profitable business.

It is important for you to consider your organization's overall relational status at this point in *Corporate Family Matters*. Just because you have a good business now doesn't mean it will always stay that way. As a leader, you must *internally* and *intentionally* strive to achieve the goals of your business plan while simultaneously developing the men and women who comprise your Corporate Family in order to maintain a productive and profitable business. Then, and only then, will you be on your way to finding the success you'd like and be able to eventually leave behind a legacy that will last. And if your company is struggling, now is the time to pinpoint those areas that must be improved upon so that relationships can be strengthened and the Corporate Family can experience unity.

> Corporate divorce includes circumstances when someone decides to leave or is asked to leave.

With that in mind, this doesn't mean divorce won't happen inside your organization. Corporate divorce includes circumstances when someone decides to leave or is asked to leave. In a sense, these types of splits will occur throughout a company's lifetime on a regular basis. In fact, sometimes these separations are the best thing that can occur in an organization. If an individual doesn't belong in your Corporate Family, he or she needs to move on for everyone's benefit. And as we will see in Chapter 8, when you clarify your Corporate Culture, certain employees will need or desire "free agency" because they no longer fit into your Corporate Family's way of doing business.

So, divorce happens…but so does remarriage. And new family members should be individuals who are not only Hall of Fame players but are also men and women who meld into your Corporate Family (we detail the attributes of Hall of Fame Leadership in *The Leading Edge*). This means that parents and siblings should be part of the hiring process for quality assurance purposes, and the requirements of the corporate family must be discussed in advance of any new hire.

Like many new relationships, remember that there usually is a terrific honeymoon period after which everyone settles back into reality. Men and women are human, so no matter how

> Helping newer members of the family learn how to fulfill their roles and responsibilities is what being a family is all about!

good your new employees seem at first, each new hire will have flaws and foibles just like the rest of us. *Exceptional leaders set high expectations for everyone, but they also regularly and consistently develop the skill sets and habits of all employees.* Helping newer members of the family learn how to fulfill their roles and responsibilities is what being a family is all about! Therefore, the more proactive and intentional your leadership is, the better your chances are of developing high-performing individuals and teams.

Additional members to your Corporate Family can also come by way of mergers and acquisitions. Sometimes these legal unions are mutually agreed upon, while others may seem more like arranged marriages. No matter the reason for the amalgamation, it's important for leaders to realize that often the parents are the ones making the choice to unite, while the children of these "blended corporate families" must go along for the ride. Some family members may be excited about the change, but others will not be. In fact, these types of remarriages and/or adoptions can create a lot of pain if not handled correctly.

> It's important for leaders to realize that often the parents are the ones making the choice to unite, while the children of these "blended corporate families" must go along for the ride.

This is where two major aspects of the Leadership Continuum must be addressed. These essential aspects are broken down into the following continuums:

Continuum #1: Rigid ⟫⟫⟫⟫⟫⟫ **Flexible**

Continuum #2: Disengaged ⟫⟫⟫⟫⟫ **Enmeshed**

In the first continuum, leaders of corporate families range from being completely rigid in their leadership style and the way they relate to others to being overly flexible. Rigidity includes a "my way or the highway" mentality, especially when it comes to newer members of the corporate family. Frequently, these leaders view those who join the company as new hires or through mergers and acquisitions as "add-ons" who must fit into the organization or leave. On the other end of this continuum are leaders who lack the ability to set boundaries and can become overwhelmed by what to do with their corporate families as they become more blended over time. They favor group genius, affiliation, and entrepreneurialism, while failing to give clear guidelines and directives. All too often, they don't provide clarity on specific roles and responsibilities.

Obviously exceptional leaders should strive for balance between the two extremes of Continuum #1, especially in regard to the development of newer corporate family members. You and your leadership team should be actively involved in their integration into the company without strangling their creativeness and innovation.

> We encourage leaders to recognize that people require their attention—and corporate family members must have clear direction, especially when it comes to achieving company goals and objectives.

The same is true about balancing the second continuum. Some leaders are disengaged when it comes to directing their companies, which can lead to a loss of productivity. You probably have experienced the kind of leaders we're talking about. They usually have separate office space, typically on a different floor from the rest of the corporate family. The only way to access them is through many layers of the assistants who insulate them, though you might be lucky enough to catch a glimpse of these aloof executives at an important corporate event or the holiday party. This sort of leader's disengagement isn't merely physical; they're usually out of touch with the men and women who work in and run their companies. We encourage leaders to recognize that people require their attention—and corporate family members must have clear direction, especially when it comes to achieving company goals and objectives.

On the other hand, employees don't want leaders to be involved in every detail of their corporate lives. Enmeshed leaders have poor boundaries, sometimes bringing their personal problems to work on a consistent basis. While we may laugh at the antics of the boss in the television show, *The Office*, unfortunately there are way too many "Michaels" in today's organizations. In addition to having bad boundaries, they waste time (theirs and others) and fail to hold others accountable. Once again, finding the balance point in this continuum is essential for good leadership as well as the ultimate success of your Corporate Family. Don't be too distant or overly-involved; instead, role-model exceptional leadership by keeping in touch with your Corporate Family and guiding them toward the goals of the business plan.

> Tomorrow won't be like today, and your organization can't ever stay the same.

Over the years, we've heard many executives and employees complain about changes in their companies. Sometimes, these individuals want the impossible: "I wish our organization would just stay exactly the way it is now!" Guess what—that's never going to happen! Tomorrow won't be like today, and your organization can't ever stay the same. *It shouldn't stay the same.* Each day ought to be a progression toward something bigger, better, and brighter for everyone involved in your Corporate Family.

> Corporate families— like all families—are dynamic, not static.

Corporate families—like all families—are dynamic, not static. They are fluid entities that can and should adjust with changing times, new advances, societal shifts, and global needs. So, as members and leaders of our corporate families, we must understand this fluid and ever-changing aspect of "family life" and help everyone in our care attain the skills needed to adjust to these transformations too.

> Healthy and successful blended families not only have parents who are balanced in the two leadership continuums, but they also have leaders who help everyone in the family make good transitions.

Healthy and successful blended families not only have parents who are balanced in the two leadership continuums, but they also have leaders who help everyone in the family make good transitions. The path to smooth transitions is a six-step process:

Step 1: The leaders of the family set clear expectations for how the family will interact and operate on a daily basis. This involves communicating a vision, establishing a mission, setting core values, and developing a business plan that everyone is aware of and agrees to. The family is both aligned and attuned. (See *The Corporate Family Covenant* at the end of this book for more ideas on how to set clear expectations).

Step 2: *Clear communication is the rule, not the exception.* When changes are forthcoming, everyone in the Corporate Family is apprised of them and can openly express any concerns.

Step 3: Parents and siblings intentionally help new members adjust to the blended Corporate Family. Procedures and policies are in place to aide with these transitions, yet there is flexibility due to differences in the personalities involved.

> **Step 4:** Conflict is guaranteed to happen, especially as employees experience shifts in power and control (see Chapter 4). Leaders must role-model conflict resolution skills and cascade these throughout their organization.

> **Step 5:** Leadership sets realistic expectations about transition time and adjustments in the Corporate Family. Regular and consistent encouragement is given to colleagues and subordinates as they fulfill respective roles and responsibilities.

> **Step 6:** Family time is scheduled in order to build bonds, create unity, and celebrate successes. "Face time" should be organized regularly and consistently.

> Clear communication is the rule, not the exception.

Making smooth transitions is a lofty goal, but not an unattainable one. As a leader, these steps require you to keep the relationships of your current and future family members a priority. As your Corporate Family members positively interact, recognize their similarities and differences, and understand they are integral to one another's success, greater levels of satisfaction will be experienced by all. Whether large or small, start-up or established, your business is an organic entity that will never be static—and, hopefully, never status quo. So keep going, and keep growing! Most of all, keep giving your all to the men and women who make up your unique Corporate Family.

> Whether large or small, start-up or established, your business is an organic entity that will never be static—and, hopefully, never status quo.

FAMILY TIME

1. Historically, how has your leadership managed the "divorces" in your Corporate Family?

2. How are "remarriages" managed in your Corporate Family?

3. Where do you fall on the two Leadership Continuums? Survey people in your sphere of influence to see how they think you are doing.

4. Does the reality of divorce and remarriage in your Corporate Family need to be addressed better? How do you equip your employees to deal with these types of transitions? What changes would you make to your organization based upon the recommendations in this chapter?

Chapter S E V E N

The Circle of Life

There seems to be a kind of order in the universe, in the movement of the stars and the turning of the earth and the changing of the seasons, and even in the cycle of human life.

Katherine Anne Porter

By the way Derek's hands were fidgeting with his coffee cup, we could tell something was wrong. The emotion on his face soon confirmed our suspicions, and it didn't take long for this COO to open up about his dilemma.

"I've been with this company twenty years next month, and I'm tired. No one seems to appreciate all of the hard work I put in around here, and our CEO is the most difficult man I've ever dealt with. I can't believe corporate hired him! He makes everyone miserable, and then they come complaining to me throughout the day. I can only take so much! I've simply got to get out of here!"

Derek went on to explain other work-related issues that were bothering him, including the new CEO's decision to reduce salaries across the board—except his own—even though the projections for business and profits appeared promising for the upcoming year. He had also asked Derek to announce this decision to all three hundred and fifteen employees. In addition to these work-related stresses, both of Derek's kids were now away at school, which left him and his wife with an empty house and two, large college tuitions.

The anxiety, angst, and anger Derek felt are not uncommon for a person his age. In fact, some might say that he stood at the brink of a mid-life crisis. Yet this crisis wasn't simply personal, it also happened to be professional. His frustrations represent only one of the many seasons experienced by men and women as they make their way through the Circle of Life.

> The Circle of Life is a unique phenomenon.

The Circle of Life is a unique phenomenon. We are born and then begin to grow and develop through various stages. From childhood to adolescence to young and then mature adulthood, people change physically, mentally, spiritually, and emotionally. Certain roles and responsibilities are taken on throughout these different periods, for instance, attending school during childhood and adolescence versus parenting and even grandparenting during adulthood.

> This Circle of Life doesn't happen only in our personal lives.

And this Circle of Life doesn't happen only in our personal lives. We move through distinct phases in our professional lives too, and these stages bring unique experiences that impact the present and the future. The

> The earliest period of our professional lives is the Start-up Phase.

earliest period of our professional lives is the ***Start-up Phase***. This is the time we dedicate to acquiring the skills necessary for the work we aspire to do, perhaps for the rest of our careers. Typically, men and women seek to equip themselves through three avenues:

1. Business, College, or University Degrees
2. Vocational Schools
3. Apprenticeship Programs and Trade Schools

Sometimes a combination of these options is required for specific professions, and time, energy, and effort must be allotted for this important developmental phase. Certain parts of this season are fun, much like those more carefree days of childhood, but others can be challenging. Some of the restlessness experienced by those in the Start-up Phase is quite similar to the angst of young people as they prepare to leave their parents' care and enter the real world.

> Once in our careers, most of us relish the initial feelings of freedom of the Stabilization Phase only to soon realize that much more learning needs to be done.

Once in our careers, most of us relish the initial feelings of freedom of the ***Stabilization Phase*** only to soon realize that much more learning needs to be done. If we're fortunate, we have good mentors during these early days of our professional lives. Some, however, aren't so fortunate. A difficult or overly-demanding boss can put a damper on the Stabilization Phase of professional experiences. Those novice days can also be fraught with frustration due to a disengaged or enmeshed leader at the helm of the corporate family (see Chapter 6).

Practice is the key to expertise.

Yet after years of effort, professionals eventually gain their ten thousand hours of practice that lead to competence in their field. Whether an architect, a contractor, a lawyer, a teacher, a doctor, or a plumber, these hours of hands-on experience are what allow a person to become an expert in his or her respective profession. Practice is the key to expertise.

This mature stage of your professional career continues to involve development, which is why it is called the Growth Phase.

This expertise is critical as you move from being a Corporate Family member in your organization to becoming an exceptional leader. In other words, your efforts in the Stabilization Phase of your career will allow you to grow and develop from sibling status to the role of parent and guardian of the entire Corporate Family. This mature stage of your professional career continues to involve development, which is why it is called the **Growth Phase**. While you have acquired a position of importance, your professional achievements have not ended simply because you have attained "leadership" status.

Your professional achievements have not ended simply because you have attained "leadership" status.

But restlessness can occur during this on-going Growth Phase, and this is exactly where Derek found himself in his professional journey. He'd been working for the same company for two decades, and he was weary of the daily grind. He also felt underappreciated (a very dangerous professional pitfall that we discuss in *The Leading Edge)* and overly-burdened by the demands of a bad boss and needy corporate family members. Derek's initial reaction is not atypical: he wanted out! He felt like the only option that would preserve his sanity was to jettison his job, seek out something new, and hopefully find some sort of satisfaction elsewhere.

Does this reaction sound like a mid-life crisis you've heard about? The problem is that the individuals who leave their families (personal and/or professional) usually find that the problems they hoped to escape exist everywhere. The grass isn't any greener! Most experts believe that it's far easier to deal with the current dilemma than attempt to avoid it, because new people bring their own set of issues, and often these will include the very ones we'd hoped to run from. But if we learn how to directly address problems now, we'll be more prepared to handle whatever comes our way in the future.

> New people bring their own set of issues, and often these will include the very ones we'd hoped to run from.

Fortunately, Derek finally came to this conclusion as well. He realized that he had invested too much of his time and energy into his current corporate family to simply give up on them, or himself. He took his role and responsibilities as parent/leader seriously, so he was willing to do more work if that's what it would take to make it through this rough patch in his professional journey. He stood at a crossroad, and rather than starting down a new path, he chose to stay the course even though he knew it wouldn't be easy with the CEO breathing down his neck.

As the LEADon team continued to work with Derek and his co-workers, we re-emphasized the three phases of the professional journey with the entire corporate family. We asked them to determine which stage they considered themselves to be in:

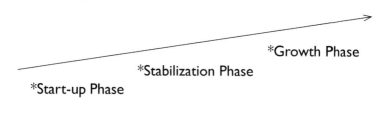

*Growth Phase

*Stabilization Phase

*Start-up Phase

Interestingly enough, not just individuals, but every organization goes through these identical developmental stages. So at any given time, you will have individuals and businesses at various phases of the Circle of Life. For instance, Derek and his corporate family belonged to a successful seventy-five-year-old business. The company had long since been through its Start-up and Stabilization Phases and was now in the Growth Phase. Yet the corporate family was comprised of people in all three stages. Derek had several interns, apprentices, and numerous employees in the Start-up and Stabilization Phases of their careers. Even within the executive team, leaders noted they were in various peaks and valleys of the Growth Phase.

> Every organization goes through these identical developmental stages.

Stop for a few minutes and consider your Circle of Life. Where are you personally? How are you progressing along life's journey? Are you feeling successful and satisfied in your personal endeavors, or are you relating to the frustrations inherent in a particular phase?

Next, consider your professional journey. In which of the three phases do you find yourself? What have been some of the highlights of your Circle of Life thus far? Are there tough times that you remember? If so, what did you learn from those periods in your profession? How have they made you a better person and Corporate Family leader? What successes have you had? Have you celebrated these?

Finally, consider your company and its current stage in the Circle of Life. Is it a Start-up that's still struggling to find its niche in the marketplace? If your business is in the Stabilization Phase, how can you make certain that the vision, mission, and goals are being met? Maybe your business is well-established, yet how might you ensure that it doesn't become stagnant? How will you keep your Corporate Family growing and developing for years to come? This continual development is extremely important if you and your company hope to achieve organizational dynasty status.

> Maybe your business is well-established, yet how might you ensure that it doesn't become stagnant? How will you keep your Corporate Family growing and developing for years to come?

This last question was one that Derek and his corporate family members had to consider. Even though one of the "parents" wasn't completely on board with how most of the family wanted to proceed, they made a decision to continue on the path toward success, together striving to reconcile their differences and work toward their business goals and objectives, no matter what obstacles lay in their path.

At LEADon, we have experienced all aspects of this Circle of Life with the leaders, teams, and organizations we've been privileged to work with. Some have been in the Start-up Phase, like a construction company founded by three friends with a vision for their industry. While each of these parents/leaders of their corporate family are in various stages of their professional Growth Phase, they're committed to put in the

> They're also dedicated to creating a great culture so that their corporate family members can successfully move through their own professional life cycles.

time and effort necessary to build their new business into something better than they ever experienced. They're also dedicated to creating a great culture so that their corporate family members can successfully move through their own professional life cycles.

Perhaps one of the best examples of professional development LEADon has seen so far is a leader named Dave. As a chief executive nearing retirement, Dave could have rested on his past achievements and comfortably cruised through the last few years of his corporate contract. But this particular leader refused to accept the status quo, even though his organization was extremely productive and profitable despite some generational issues within the corporate family.

These seemingly minor disputes were what troubled Dave, and, as a seasoned leader, he recognized that they could become more significant issues once he was gone. So Dave asked LEADon for guidance with the mounting generational dilemma and sibling rivalry (look over Chapters 4 and 5 again to review these concepts if needed). He also wanted assistance in strengthening the current corporate family and preparing leaders for their future parental roles and responsibilities (see Chapter 3).

So the team at LEADon presented generational workshops for the entire corporate family, greatly improving their professional skill sets, and we also helped Dave select a group of qualified corporate siblings to receive specific leadership development, preparing them for the role of parenting the corporate family. As all of the teams began to grow and develop, opportunities arose for different departments to work toward becoming more aligned and attuned. Eventually barriers were broken down between operations, sales, supply chain, field, and service teams. The end result went beyond expectations, and Dave's successor was so motivated by these experiences that he continued to utilize LEADon's internal and intentional leadership development within the corporate family.

> Dave recognized the golden nugget about success that we're trying to pass on to you: the Corporate Family Matters!

Even toward the end of his professional Circle of Life, Dave recognized the golden nugget about success that we're trying to pass on to you: the Corporate Family Matters! What you do to develop your own professional skill sets and habits *will* make a difference—now and for your future legacy. How you help all of your Corporate Family members acquire the skills they need to be successful will impact them, your business, and the bottom line in exponential ways.

> How you help all of your Corporate Family members acquire the skills they need to be successful will impact them, your business, and the bottom line in exponential ways.

We know this because we've seen the success stories over and over again. We've also experienced them right along with leaders like you who recognize that, as everyone moves through the Circle of Life, how we choose to journey through it makes all the difference in the overall success and satisfaction we experience during our occupational years.

FAMILY TIME

1. Personally, where are you in the Circle of Life? Are you satisfied with your successes thus far, and what more do you hope to accomplish?

2. Where are you in the journey of your professional Circle of Life? What are you doing to continue growing and developing?

3. How about your Corporate Family? Where does it fall in the Circle of Life we've been discussing? How do you plan to keep it thriving now…and in the future?

4. Think about and review your personal and professional Circle of Life. What does your legacy look like? Should you make changes to ensure a Circle of Life and legacy that you're proud of? Make a list of your positive strengths. Next, make a list of midcourse corrections you need to make in order to leave a meaningful and lasting legacy.

Creating a New Corporate Family History

If I were to try to read, much less answer, all the attacks made on me, this shop might as well be closed for any other business. I do the very best I know how—the very best I can, and I mean to keep doing so until the end.

Abraham Lincoln

Connie Martinez could hardly believe what she was hearing. And, as she looked around the room, most of the other executive team members were nodding their heads in agreement as the CFO summed up his ideas for cutbacks in their organization in order to increase profits and dividends for stock holders.

Connie knew that many of these changes would dramatically impact the corporate family, especially when it came to overall morale. She'd worked too hard during the past three years since she'd been hired to improve communication and corporate spirit throughout this large company to let it get wiped away in one whisk of the CFO's fiscal eraser.

"Ted, I think you've got some good ideas for improving our prospects for profitability this year, but I believe we should take time to discuss the unseen costs such adjustments might also incur."

Twelve sets of eyes quickly shifted her direction, several with eyebrows raised. Few seasoned team members ever questioned Ted's initiatives, let alone someone relatively new to the corporate family. But a lengthy discussion did follow, thanks in part to the support of the CEO who'd hired Connie and had witnessed firsthand the positive changes she'd made in their organization. At the end of the meeting, Connie felt satisfied that some of the proposed cuts had been revised.

> **Good business extends beyond the bottom line!**

Connie's type of thinking is the sort that separates ordinary businesses from those that go on to become organizational dynasties. *Good business extends beyond the bottom line!* Sure, profitability is great, but the people involved are the ones who make the whole process possible. And changing your Corporate Family history must include considering how the overall culture impacts everything you and your colleagues do—both now and in the future.

> **Changing your Corporate Family history must include considering how the overall culture impacts everything you and your colleagues do—both now and in the future.**

In *The Leading Edge*, we delve into current research that supports the concept that corporate culture positively impacts productivity and profitability. We've also seen this reality in every organization we've worked with over the years. Good cultures make for great business. And bad cultures? Well, suffice it to say that they always impact the bottom line, as well.

If you truly want to change your Corporate Family history for the better, then, as an exceptional leader, you must help to clarify your specific corporate culture. *If you don't define your culture, the culture will define you.* In order to have an outstanding organization—one that's striving for dynasty status—then you must internally and intentionally set the standards of the culture you hope to experience now and eventually leave as your legacy.

> If you don't define your culture, the culture will define you.

At LEADon, we describe culture as the foundation for everything you and your co-workers do. It is composed of three distinct components:

1. **Values**: the principles, goals, or standards held and accepted by a group of people.
2. **Beliefs:** statements or virtues that people accept as true.
3. **Behavior Patterns:** specific actions that relay general character, state of mind, or response to circumstances.

In your organization, the Values, Beliefs, and Behavior Patterns your Corporate Family accept and acknowledge as true depict who you are and what you are about. As you consider your company, how do you feel about the principles, goals, and values that you and your colleagues strive for? What kind of beliefs do your co-workers, clients, and even competition have about your business? And, finally, do the behavior patterns of your Corporate Family members represent something that you're proud to be part of? If not, what needs to change?

> Corporate culture is fluid and dynamic. It is malleable. It has more to do with the commonality of people rather than where they've come from.

The wonderful news about culture is that it can and should change! *Corporate culture is fluid and dynamic. It is malleable. It has more to do with the commonality of people rather than where they've come from.* This is especially good news for companies that have been struggling with a difficult family history. Sometimes the negative history may have been created due to poor leadership. It could also have been caused by corrupt, divisive, or destructive corporate family members. In other instances, change may simply need to occur because of transitions in the marketplace. Questions should be raised when things don't seem to fit the current culture. Connie Martinez knew that just because the CFO's initiatives had always been accepted in the past didn't mean they were right for the present-day corporate family.

> **One of the most challenging forces that the leaders/ parents of today's corporate families face is the culture in which we live.**

One of the most challenging forces that the leaders/ parents of today's corporate families face is the culture in which we live. Sadly, there is a culture clash being played out in society, one unlike any we've experienced before in the history of the United States. The two diametrically opposed ends of this struggle are Victimization and Entitlement, and Personal Responsibility.

Victimization & Entitlement 《《《《《《《《《《《《◈》》》》》》》》》》》》 **Personal Responsibility**

An individual who is closer to the Victimization end of the clash within today's culture views life from a "poor me" perspective. Members of this group feel that they've been victimized in numerous ways, from difficult lives at home to stresses of living, past wrongs, or future uncertainties. Those in the Entitlement group believe that, by virtue of their mere existence, they're owed something—maybe even everything. They firmly contend that, since everyone is created equal, things should be distributed equally, without respect to equity in responsibility.

This clash has subtly (and sometimes not-so-subtly) impacted the culture of business across America and around the globe. Whereas Personal Responsibility was once the norm, now companies must contend with an employee pool that has different expectations. For the United States, a nation that was built upon basic rights that *can lead* to multiple opportunities, the work ethic upon which we found our past strength suddenly seems rather shaky in light of a generation of employees reared to "expect" and not always give. This polarization of cultural values is at odds with the history of the land of opportunity that our founding fathers and mothers lived and died for.

> Leaders/parents must take the initiative to define the current culture of their organizations for the stability of the entire corporate family.

In spite of these external forces, leaders/ parents must take the initiative to define the current culture of their organizations for the stability of the entire corporate family. They must also get the buy-in of corporate family members—from senior team members (parents) to all employees (siblings). Everyone on staff must show deference to the principles the corporate family chooses to unite around. There must also be agreement in how they will apply those principles day in and day out.

> Whenever clear-cut boundaries are established, resistance is bound to occur.

This brings us to a point where we must offer some words of caution. *Whenever clear-cut boundaries are established, resistance is bound to occur.* This is as true in our professional relationships as it is in our personal ones. What does a toddler do when you put up a security gate that is clearly for his or her protection? The child invariably tries to go right through it. And how about teenagers? Do they jump for joy as soon as you establish a new rule—even if it's in their best interest? Of course not! This resistance is equally strong in adulthood. For instance, if the speed limit is set at sixty-five miles per hour, many adults will push this boundary line to seventy, seventy-five, or even eighty! The automatic acceptance of what is good, safest, and best isn't always a natural part of humanity's skill sets.

> Once specific guidelines are established, some individuals realize that their lack of commitment to the family will be discovered.

Boundaries must be established, nonetheless. And those defined guidelines must be enforced. So whether in your personal or professional life, when someone decides to defy the culture as defined by the entire family, consequences should follow. This is what we describe as accountability.

The bottom line? Anticipate resistance and even outright rebellion by some people, and possible abandonment of the family by others. There will always be a few members in any society that simply refuse to play by the rules. Once specific guidelines are established, some individuals realize that their lack of commitment to the family will be discovered. And frankly, it's better for everyone if these individuals seek "free agency" anyway. While we work to keep the family together, men and women have the freedom to choose.

The wide array of corporate cultures in the national and international organizations that LEADon has worked with can be sorted into four specific categories:

1. ***The Destructive Corporate Culture***: These types of corporate families typically have divisive leaders embedded throughout the organizational chart. There is a "revolving door" effect when it comes to retention of employees, as healthy individuals often leave, while bad citizens remain. Sometimes these businesses are surprisingly profitable; sometimes they're not. What they do have in common is that no one has been willing to change the history of corporate chaos.

2. ***The Status Quo Corporate Culture***: These companies are composed of people who are comfortable with "okay." They're okay with average performance, average productivity, and average profitability. Leaders and staff alike are oblivious to culture. These organizations thrive or dive depending on the leadership that's in power because they have no strong, cultural foundation to support them in difficult times.

3. ***The Hypocritical Corporate Culture***: Organizations in this classification "talk the talk, but don't walk the walk." They have a vision, a mission statement, and even a set of core values—many of which can be seen on pens, notepaper, T-shirts, and banners. The problem is that few members of the corporate family really adhere to them, and clients and business associates alike could recount story after story of their hypocritical behavior patterns.

4. ***The Healthy Corporate Culture***: Businesses who fall into this final category are the gold standard in their respective industries. Competitors strive to be like them, and clients consider them a "value buy." These organizations have a clearly defined culture that is embraced and supported by all members of the corporate family. Yet this culture is also dynamic, fluid, and evolving so that it can

develop everybody to become who they need to be in the corporate family. The environment of these companies is positive, productive, and profitable because of sound Values, Beliefs, and Behavior Patterns.

> As a leader, will you take responsibility for helping to define your corporate culture—or will you let it define you?

Obviously our goal is for you and your organization to be firmly established in this fourth category. If that isn't the situation right now, take heart! Remember, cultures can and do change. So how can you begin to transform your Corporate Family and start creating a new legacy? To begin, you must consider a few clarifying questions:

1. What does your corporate culture currently look like to you and to others?
2. How is your corporate culture impacting the bottom line?
3. As a leader, will you take responsibility for helping to define your corporate culture—or will you let it define you?
4. Are you willing to intentionally improve the culture of your organization—and include all corporate family members in the process?

The team at LEADon always stresses that leadership must be *internal* and *intentional*.

> Leadership must be internal and intentional.

What do we mean by this? *Internal* has to do with you, the exceptional leader, first; then it moves to your current Corporate Family members. New habits and skills sets must be worked on by you, the leader;

then they can be cascaded throughout your entire organization. Second, this effort must be *intentional.* You can't hope it will happen or believe that one day you'll have time to get to it. That intentionality must start now. And notice that internal and intentional both begin with "I." *I* need to be committed to putting these strategies into practice, and *I* must be dedicated to my Corporate Family's current and future success.

> *I* need to be committed to putting these strategies into practice, and *I* must be dedicated to my Corporate Family's current and future success.

The internal and intentional effort needed to clarify the Values, Beliefs, and Behavior Patterns of your business will require time and energy. Creating a new Corporate Family history will also involve a "conscious competence," or a working knowledge about your corporate culture and how it will be experienced by your family members. You can no longer afford to *think* you've got a good culture; you need to *know* you do. Employees shouldn't merely feel things are okay in your organization, they should be able to explain the various components of your outstanding corporate culture. And everyone—from colleagues to clients—must be able to experience the positive impact of cultural and corporate change.

> Everyone—from colleagues to clients—must be able to experience the positive impact of cultural and corporate change.

Exceptional leaders keep going! They keep creating and developing, even if it means fighting against unseen forces or seemingly intangible foes. That's the kind of fortitude those who founded our country had, and it's the same kind of determination it will take to leave your own unforgettable legacy.

FAMILY TIME

1. Describe your current corporate culture. What are the Values, Beliefs, and Behavior Patterns that explain what your organization is all about?

2. What aspects of the culture of your company need to be changed? Why? How can you and your team begin to implement these improvements?

3. What are some positive characteristics of your Corporate Family history? Have you celebrated these attributes? How would you like to see this history transform for the benefit of future Corporate Family members?

4. What challenges does today's culture present to you, your colleagues, and your organization? How can you address any cultural clashes as you and your Corporate Family move into the future?

Legacy and the Organizational Dynasty

No matter what you've done for yourself or for humanity, if you can't look back on having given love and attention to your own family, what have you really accomplished?
Lee Iacocca, former CEO and Chairman of Chrysler

If you had asked people in the 1970s about the Chrysler Corporation's prospects for the future, many would have replied in similar ways:

"Doomed."

"Totally done."

"Going the way of the dinosaur!"

For a variety of reasons, including troubling economic times for carmakers and anti-trust laws, Chrysler even had to appeal to the government to avoid bankruptcy. However in 1979, a tipping point came for this corporate family. A former Ford executive, named Lee Iacocca, became CEO. Under his visionary leadership, the Chrysler Corporation not only revived but also began to thrive.

While the entire corporate family of Chrysler was involved in the remarkable rebound, they were able to change their history because they could rally around one extraordinary individual's leadership. Indeed, because of his tenacity and fortitude, Iacocca has become iconic in American business lore. Recently, we saw his picture gracing the cover of a national magazine. He looked confident and completely satisfied—and amazingly vibrant at eighty-five-years-young!

What is the key to Iacocca's outstanding legacy of success? While we could identify many of his positive leadership qualities, we believe a major factor is Iacocca's focus on family. He has pointed out this belief about the importance of family repeatedly, and the LEADon team couldn't agree more. *Exceptional leaders place a priority on their personal families as well as their professional ones.* This life balance is essential because home is where we first hone our leadership skills, building the family units that will carry on our personal legacy for generations to come (we recommend you read Chapter 4, Discovering Personal and Professional Life Balance, in *The Leading Edge* for additional insights on this topic).

> Exceptional leaders place a priority on their personal families as well as their professional ones.

This is a good time to reflect on your personal and professional leadership. How have you been doing in keeping both of these in balance? Are there areas that need improvement? Where have you experienced success? Have you celebrated theses victories? (We'll talk more about the importance of celebrations in Chapter 10).

We're not asking you to be an expert in all areas of leadership right now. As we've pointed out, leadership development is a process that happens over time. *Exceptional leaders need to be continually working at expertise, pressing on toward their goals and dreams for the future.* Becoming an outstanding leader is all about the journey, and how you choose to travel down this road of personal and professional development will make all of the difference in your overall legacy.

> Exceptional leaders need to be continually working at expertise, pressing on toward their goals and dreams for the future.

Thinking about legacy is important throughout our lives, not just toward the end of our careers. Focusing on our long-term legacy helps us picture the final finish line that, for some, may be way down the road, but is influenced by our actions *now*. It is also essential for us to consider the type of personal and professional legacy we hope to attain so we can make "midcourse corrections—" those adjustments in approach and attitude that allow us to keep achieving no matter what life dishes up. So, considering what you want your legacy to be is essential for current and future success.

> Considering what you want your legacy to be is essential for current and future success.

We have some good news and bad news about legacy. Let's start with the bad news: *you will always struggle when it comes to creating, developing, and maintaining your family.* Here are some reasons for this reality:

+ Every family has blessings and burdens (Chapter 1).
+ Each corporation deals with its own share of family secrets (Chapter 2).
+ Parents are never perfect (Chapter 3).
+ Where there are siblings, there will be rivalry (Chapter 4).

✦ Corporate families will always have generational and gender issues (Chapter 5).

✦ Divorce happens, as well as remarriage and the resulting blended family experiences (Chapter 6).

✦ Individuals and corporate families simultaneously move through the Circle of Life (Chapter 7).

✦ Corporate culture requires constant cultivation and support (Chapter 8).

So, what's the good news? All of the above! Now that you are aware of these crucial components of your Corporate Family, you can work on them. You have full disclosure as to what problems you're currently facing, plus some specific strategies to directly engage any area of concern. And you're not alone. This phenomenon is common to all of us in the workforce!

> The other piece of great news is that all behaviors and cultural nuances are *learned*—and if something is learned, it can be changed.

The other piece of great news is that all behaviors and cultural nuances are *learned*—and if something is learned, it can be changed. For instance, just because the parents of your organization have not been unified in the past doesn't mean that pattern has to continue forever. You can change it. *You have to change it!* If your colleagues and staff are behaving more like enemies than family members, then you must address this dysfunctional situation and strive to improve those sibling relationships.

> Who knows, perhaps, like Iacocca, you'll even take your company from potential dinosaur to organizational dynasty!

We're not saying this process will be easy or painless. No doubt, there were many days when Lee Iacocca wondered what on earth he'd gotten himself into. Perhaps he thought about the comfortable job he'd left at Ford, wishing he could return to that corporate family and cruise into retirement. Had he chosen the easy path, the mention of his name would have a different reaction today. *Iacocca—who?*

> Part of being an exceptional leader is preparing for your eventual absence.

Maybe you can relate. Perhaps you're in a company that is struggling to survive. The economy has left you nothing but downward trending sales, a discouraged Corporate Family, and a dismal forecast for the future. Or it could be that your organization is financially stable, but you've got a family that's fragmented and dysfunctional. Whatever your circumstances, they can improve with internal and intentional effort. Who knows, perhaps, like Iacocca, you'll even take your company from potential dinosaur to organizational dynasty!

> Great companies are always in the process of preparing the outstanding leaders of tomorrow.

In order to accomplish this, we have one more essential aspect of legacy that must be addressed: *Succession.* Part of being an exceptional leader is preparing for your eventual absence. Even if you are relatively new to your company, in your professional prime, or simply young at heart, no one lasts forever. Great companies are always in the process of preparing the outstanding leaders of tomorrow.

> Life is full of the unexpected.

Training future leaders is particularly important because life is full of the unexpected. Take, for example, the life of Major General Robert Ross. Never heard of him? We're not surprised. We hadn't either until we reviewed the history of the War of 1812.

Robert Ross was born into a military family. He worked his way through the ranks of the British Army to take command of the twentieth regiment. After many battles in the Napoleonic Wars, he was given the assignment to sail to the United States and foil the young country's attempts at autonomy. After successfully assisting in the burning of Washington, D.C., the general led his troops toward Baltimore. Yet at the Battle of North Point the unexpected happened: a sniper hit and fatally wounded this seasoned leader.

Historians report that this singular event proved to be a huge blow to the British, especially in the morale of the troops. The line of succession wasn't adequately prepared, and Ross' replacement didn't command the same respect from the soldiers. Of all people, Major General Robert Ross should have known better, because he had been seriously wounded just before receiving his orders to go to America, barely recovering in time to make the journey.

> While no one wants to think about the worst, exceptional leaders prepare for these circumstances anyway!

What if a carefully devised succession plan had been in place? What if Ross had been developing the leadership skills of his subordinates, just in case? What if the rest of the "family" had experienced the leadership of his replacements, learning to trust their abilities and build rapport with these future leaders? If more strategic effort had been made in these areas, perhaps the British would have been the victors.

While no one wants to think about the worst, exceptional leaders prepare for these circumstances anyway! They know their corporate family members need a smooth transition, whenever the need arises, in order for productivity and profitability to continue in the future. In addition, they realize that future leaders *must be equipped* in order to be ready to assume the roles and responsibilities of leading/parenting the corporate family.

So, what are you doing to prepare current and future leaders of your Corporate Family? Are you developing "bench strength?" Bench strength, in sports terminology, means that you have leaders-in-waiting, so that when the starters are sidelined (and they often will be), competent replacements can step in and help lead the team to victory. The more ability, expertise, and depth you have on the bench, the better your chances are of succeeding in the short- and long-term. And the long-term effect is what will determine both your legacy as well as that of your Corporate Family.

Several years ago, we met with the leader of a company who was toying with the idea of leadership development. He'd started a business on his own, which now, thirty years later, had grown into a 100 million dollar-a-year organization with more than one hundred and fifty employees. As he was nearing an age during which he wanted to work less and travel more, he became concerned about his succession plan. And he had reasons to be worried. The four "leaders" who wanted to take over the company weren't prepared to do so. One had inherited his position simply because he'd married into the family, and he had little knowledge or ability about how to lead a corporate family.

Plus, the corporate family was a chaotic mess. There was infighting, backstabbing, and general dislike among many employees. No process for conflict resolution was in place, even though there were ample opportunities to practice those skill sets. Unfortunately, a source told us recently that this leader is still struggling with a dysfunctional organization. He decided he didn't want to add leadership development to his budget, even though the overall cost to his legacy is now far beyond the bottom-line results he'd been so focused upon. Sadly, his current legacy is a company with a negative image in the industry.

Yet the team at LEADon has witnessed numerous success stories, mostly due to competent leaders and teams who have determined to make their corporate family legacy a priority, including succession planning and discussions about legacy as part of their business planning.

Exceptional leadership is a high calling and requires a consistent focus on developing leaders for today and tomorrow. We might know Major General Robert Ross' name better than Lee Iacocca's if each man had made different decisions about future leadership. But that's history. *What you have is the present—a gift of time and opportunity.* You can keep doing what you're doing, or you can transform. You can get by with okay, or you can aim for the extraordinary. Legacy, like much of life, is about choice. What you choose will make all of the difference.

> Legacy, like much of life, is about choice. What you choose will make all of the difference.

Organizational dynasties and the legacy of their leaders don't happen by accident. There is an internal and intentional effort involved in their creation and development. The leaders care for their Corporate Families. Family members thrive in their environment and are willing to work harder than ever to ensure everyone's success. And the entire organization moves from being a mere business to becoming a true Corporate Family that does and always will matter. Now that's a legacy worth leaving.

FAMILY TIME

1. Review the "good news about legacy" bullet points which reflect upon concepts from each chapter you've read so far. Which areas represent strengths in your Corporate Family? What are some weaknesses that you've pinpointed?

2. Make a list of any areas you feel need intentional effort in the upcoming days, weeks, and months. What leaders/parents can help you implement these positive changes? What employees/siblings should also be included in this process?

3. How is your Corporate Family developing "bench strength"? What leadership development plan do you have in place for equipping future leaders?

Chapter T E N

Celebrating the Family

I celebrate myself, and sing myself, and what I assume
you shall assume, for every atom belonging to me as good
belongs to you.

Walt Whitman

As we write this book, our family is preparing for another celebration. This time, it is a college graduation, an event that has been twenty-two years in the making. Obviously, the graduate has done most of the work involved in the achievement, but he'd be the first to admit he couldn't have accomplished everything on his own. His parents provided guidance and financial assistance. Siblings and extended family members offered support and encouragement. Because of this combined, group effort, everyone is ready to celebrate.

Since this is a momentous occasion, there will be a formal ceremony full of pomp and circumstance. But there will also be other methods of merrymaking. Parties are being thrown by various college departments, and our family is planning a dinner at a local restaurant. A few gifts will be bestowed in order to commemorate this special event.

This is just one example of the ways that families can celebrate. We honor someone when he or she accomplishes something. We have times of celebration throughout the year that are unique to our specific families: birthdays, anniversaries, and religious holidays. In the United States, we also celebrate with our national family on Memorial Day, the Fourth of July, Labor Day, and Thanksgiving. From time to time, we even have surprise celebrations when something unexpected happens: an engagement is announced, a family member is having a baby, or someone gets a special award.

> The Corporate Family is composed of people, and people not only like to celebrate, they need to celebrate!

These same types of celebrations must occur in our Corporate Families, too. The Corporate Family is composed of people, and people not only like to celebrate, *they need to celebrate!* There is an innate desire within each of us to be acknowledged and appreciated. Parents learn early on that they can best motivate children if they encourage and reward good effort rather than simply punish kids for misbehavior. Research clearly suggests that positively supporting and rewarding productivity far exceeds penalizing people when it comes to desired outcomes. *Praise and positive reinforcement empower people and, in turn, fuel productivity and profitability.*

> Praise and positive reinforcement empower people and, in turn, fuel productivity and profitability.

In our personal families, empowered people perform better, and they become better individuals. This is equally true for our

Corporate Family members. When leaders learn new methods to acknowledge what employees have done and reward them in ways that are meaningful (not just monetarily), then they'll have happy, energized Corporate Family members who'll be ready to follow them and fulfill the business plan.

Have you ever wondered why some men and women can work for decades at a company and never know how much they meant to their Corporate Families until their retirement dinner? This is reality in far too many organizations. At that dinner or farewell ceremony, kind words are spoken, a watch or some token of appreciation is given, and many of these retirees hear for the first time how valuable they were to the company they're now leaving! Is it any wonder that the sincerity of that appreciation is questioned by those involved?

> Your Corporate Family members need to know right now how important they are to you and others in your company.

Leaders, retirement is way too late in the game for accolades to be given for the first time! Your Corporate Family members need to know right now how important they are to you and others in your company. They must be *regularly* and *consistently* encouraged about what they're doing that adds value to the business and to those around them. And leaders, you are the ones that must make sure this is happening! As we share in *The Leading Edge* (see Chapter 7), developing and maintaining a "Culture of Appreciation" are essential for every successful business.

> Developing and maintaining a "Culture of Appreciation" are essential for every successful business.

This is particularly true as we consider current and future trends in our companies. As we discussed in Chapter 5, the younger generations in today's workforce are motivated differently than senior members. While men and women from the Silent and Baby Boom Generations strive to achieve for achievement's sake, Gen Xers and Millennials don't roll that way. In fact, many members of these two generational groups prefer "face time" over traditional incentive plans. In other words, they value relationships and time with those they care about—including Corporate Family members.

> Every family is unique, so the types of commemorations, festivities, rites, and rituals your organization requires will be equally diverse.

You may be hoping about now that we'd provide you with a concise inventory or checklist of how appreciation and celebration should look in your organization, but it's not quite that simple. *Every family is unique, so the types of commemorations, festivities, rites, and rituals your organization requires will be equally diverse.* What we can offer you are some guidelines to establishing a pattern of celebration in your Corporate Family. Let's begin with three key components of your corporate celebrations:

1. **Established Celebrations:** These events represent important, even momentous occasions in your organization and Corporate Family. This would include the founding of your company, pivotal or poignant dates in the company history, and other days set aside for "face time." The latter should consist of quarterly calendared events when your entire Corporate Family gathers to simply enjoy one another's company, build rapport, and be encouraged about their future together. Whether this is a company picnic, holiday party, or formal corporate event, be sure you calendar these dates early and encourage all members of the Corporate Family to participate.

2. **Personal and Professional Celebrations:** Since your organization is composed of people, there will be numerous personal and professional events to recognize and celebrate throughout the year. These include birthdays, anniversaries, graduations, notable points of employment, awards, achievements, and victories. For instance, every employee's birthday can be recognized via e-newsletters with relative ease. While this may seem inconsequential to some, many men and women feel valued when this personal day is remembered. On the professional side, when an individual or team completes a project or gains a new client, their efforts should be recognized in some way, even by a simple word of praise at the weekly meeting or an after-work, happy hour event.

3. **Surprise Celebrations:** Sometimes the unexpected happens, and when the surprise is a good thing, individuals, teams, and the entire Corporate Family should have a chance to be part of the celebration. Perhaps this is an unexpected victory, such as when your company's bid turned out to be better than your competitor and you get the new contract. Maybe someone on your team receives great personal news—they're going to adopt a child or they just closed the loan on their first home. Be spontaneous. Plan some sort of celebration on the spot to commemorate the event and bring your team together.

> As a leader, one of the most significant ways you will impact your colleagues and co-workers is through small, seemingly simple acts.

As a leader, one of the most significant ways you will impact your colleagues and co-workers is through small, seemingly simple acts. **While some executives believe in that classic movie line, "It's not personal, it's business," at LEADon, we contend that it's business *and* it's personal!** If you want to empower members of your Corporate Family, you'll spend more time celebrating who they are and what they're doing than worrying how that celebration might impact the bottom line. As we point out in *The Leading Edge*, research confirms that your productivity and profitability will be better than you ever imagined by implementing these principles in your Corporate Family culture!

Take a few minutes to think about the ways you celebrate within your organization. How does your Corporate Family commemorate significant events? What is done to honor current employees' personal and professional celebrations and victories? Do your teams celebrate when they have successes? If so, how? And what about gatherings for the entire Corporate Family? Are there regular and consistent opportunities for all Corporate Family members to have face time with one another?

Throughout the years, the team at LEADon has interacted with many types of corporate families, and each one has its own, distinct culture and ways of celebrating together. Some of these organizations had fairly good practices in place to acknowledge, appreciate, and celebrate individuals, teams, and the entire corporate family. Others had good intentions about celebrating, but they often lost interest when "more pressing" concerns arose. These tend to be the companies that are also constantly struggling with chaotic and dysfunctional corporate family units.

> Remember, when people feel valued, they typically perform far beyond expectations.

Many organizations often fail to recognize and appreciate people and performance appropriately. If you're realizing that your company may fall into this under-appreciating category, then it's time to change this part of your corporate history. Your Corporate Family should be what matters most. Remember, when people feel valued, they typically perform far beyond expectations. All that's needed is more internal and intentional effort by you, the exceptional leader.

Here are a few ways that you can get this process started today and begin moving closer to creating a lasting legacy as an organizational dynasty:

+ Celebrate the fact you have a Corporate Family that's truly significant.

> Celebrate the fact you have a Corporate Family that's truly significant.

+ Celebrate that your Corporate Family is on a journey toward growth and improvement, no matter where you may have started.
+ Celebrate good leadership and the efforts to take your organization into a productive and profitable future.
+ Celebrate the fact that you've chosen to resolve conflict in meaningful and productive ways.
+ Celebrate the differences you have as a Corporate Family, and celebrate that you are discovering ways to use those differences as assets rather than liabilities.
+ Celebrate that your Corporate Family is a dynamic, fluid, and ever-changing organization!
+ Celebrate that, no matter what's happened in the past, the future is where your focus will be.

> Celebrate that your Corporate Family is a dynamic, fluid, and ever-changing organization!

+ Celebrate that you're building bench strength by internally and intentionally equipping current and future generations of leaders.

This list could go on and on. There are many aspects of your Corporate Family that you can and should celebrate. While you and your Corporate Family members are still a work in progress, you need to appreciate how far you've come as you keep focused on where you'd like to be one day. Even those that we would categorize as organizational dynasties shouldn't stop and rest on their laurels. If they do, their corporate families will become stagnant and could lose their position of professional pre-eminence. *Remember, all families, personal and professional, must keep growing and developing together in order to survive and thrive in a constantly changing world.*

> Even those that we would categorize as organizational dynasties shouldn't stop and rest on their laurels.

> All families, personal and professional, must keep growing and developing together in order to survive and thrive in a constantly changing world.

This type of united effort doesn't happen by chance, and exceptional leaders who are willing to put in internal and intentional effort are essential to this process. Organizations are truly organic—composed of human beings with skills, hopes, weaknesses, dreams, needs, and possibilities. Bringing all of these men and women together into one committed family unit may seem like a daunting task, but we're here to tell you that it's not only possible; it's imperative! Leaders who can make the leap from mere executives to caring and compassionate parents of the corporate family will be the ones who leave the kind of lasting legacy they've always dreamed about.

> Organizations are truly organic—composed of human beings with skills, hopes, weaknesses, dreams, needs, and possibilities.

At this point in history, the journey of your organization is in your hands. Some day you'll pass this important position on to another caretaker, but for now, it's up to you to decide how you will lead your Corporate Family into the future and what kind of legacy you want to leave behind. You should celebrate how far you've traveled on this personal and professional journey. Take time to assess all of your blessings, and then envision the possibilities that are awaiting you in the future. The road to success lies just ahead of you, especially now that you understand how to make your Corporate Family really matter.

> Leaders who can make the leap from mere executives to caring and compassionate parents of the corporate family will be the ones who leave the kind of lasting legacy they've always dreamed about.

FAMILY TIME

1. Does your Corporate Family have meaningful celebrations?

2. Make a list of all of the "celebratory events" that *should* take place to honor and recognize deserving Corporate Family members.

3. Create a corporate calendar for all family members to see when and where you will be celebrating various events throughout the year.

4. Now, celebrate! You've accomplished a lot and are on your way to achieving organizational dynasty status!

The Corporate Family Covenant

1. All Corporate Family Members will be valued and appreciated.

2. Our Corporate Family is the cornerstone of our business, so it will never be taken for granted or disrespected.

3. We will directly embrace all problems and provide solutions within our Corporate Family.

4. Parents will lead our Corporate Family with care and compassion.

5. Parents and Siblings will agree to resolve conflict according to the guidelines established by our Corporate Family.

6. Because our Corporate Family wants to avoid secrets, lines of communication will remain open between Parents and Siblings at all times, even when faced with conflict and adversity.

7. Corporate Family Members commit to supporting and assisting one another, especially during times of difficulty and stress.

8. Our Corporate Family will agree to mutual accountability at all times.

9. Parents will internally and intentionally equip the next generation(s) of leaders.

10. Our Corporate Family will celebrate victories together on a regular and consistent basis.

Recommended Reading

Barna, G., ed. (1997). *Leaders on Leadership.* Ventura, CA: Regal Books.

Bennis, W. (1989). *Why Leaders Can't Lead.* San Francisco: Jossey-Bass.

Blackaby, H., & Blackaby, R. (2001). *Spiritual Leadership.* Nashville: Broadman & Holman Publishers.

Blanchard, K., & Johnson, S. (1982). *The One Minute Manager.* New York: Berkley Books.

Blanchard, K., & Lorber, R. (2006). *Putting the One Minute Manager to Work: How to Turn the 3 Secrets into Skills.* New York: William Morrow and Company, Inc.

Blanchard, K., McKay, H.M., & Bowles, S. (1993). *Raving Fans: A Revolutionary Approach to Customer Service.* New York: William Morrow and Company, Inc.

Blanchard, K., Zigami, D., & Zigami, P. (1985). *Leadership and the One Minute Manager.* New York: William Morrow and Company, Inc.

Brookhiser, R. (2008). *George Washington on Leadership.* New York: Basic Books.

Burns, J.M. (1978). *Leadership.* New York: Harper Torchbooks.

Champy, J. (1995). *Reengineering Management: The Mandate for New Leadership.* New York: Harper Business.

Collins, J. C., & Porras, J.I. (1997). *Built to Last: Successful Habits of Visionary Companies.* New York: HarperBusiness.

Collins, J. (2001). *Good to Great: Why Some Companies Make the Leap and Others Don't.* New York: Harper Business.

Crocker, H. W. (1999). *Robert E. Lee on Leadership: Executive Lessons in Character, Courage, and Vision.* Rocklin, CA: Forum.

Crowley, K., & Elster, K. (2006). *Working with You is Killing Me: Freeing Yourself from Emotional Traps at Work.* New York: Business Plus.

Dupree, M. (1989). *Leadership Is an Art.* New York: Dell Publishing.

Dupree, M. (1992). *Leadership Jazz.* New York: Dell Publishing.

Deal, T.E., & Kennedy, A.A. (2000). *Corporate Cultures.* New York: Basic Books.

Drucker, P.F. (1996). *The Executives in Action.* New York: HarperBusiness.

Fullan, M. (2001). *Leading in a Culture of Change.* San Francisco: Jossey-Bass.

Gardner, H. (1995). *Leading Minds: An Anatomy of Leadership.* New York: Basic Books.

Gardner, J.W. (1990). *On Leadership.* New York: Free Press.

Garfield, C. (1987). *Peak Performers: The New Heroes of American Business.* New York: William Morrow and Company, Inc.

Gladwell, M. (2005). *Blink: The Power of Thinking without Thinking.* New York: Little, Brown & Company.

Gladwell, M. (2008). *Outliers: The Story of Success.* New York: Little, Brown and Company.

Goleman, D. (1997). *Emotional Intelligence.* New York: Bantam Books.

Goleman, D. (1998) *Working with Emotional Intelligence.* New York: Bantam Books.

Goleman, D., Boyatzis, R., & McKee, A. (2002). *Primal Leadership: Realizing the Power of Emotional Intelligence.* Boston: Harvard Business School Press.

Green, P. (1992). *Alexander of Macedon: 356-323 B.C. A Historical Biography.* Ewing, New Jersey: University of California Press.

Greenleaf, R. (1983). *Servant Leadership: A Journey into the Nature of Legitimate Power and Greatness.* New Jersey: Paulist Press.

Hamilton, J. R. (1973). *Alexander the Great.* Pittsburgh: University of Pittsburgh Press.

Hasselbein, F., Goldsmith, M., & Beckard, R., eds. (1996). *The Leader of the Future*. San Francisco: Jossey-Bass.

Haughton, L. (2004). *It's Not What You Say . . . It's What You Do: How Following Through at Every Level Can Make or Break Your Company*. New York: Currency/Doubleday.

Hayward, S.F. (1997). *Churchill on Leadership: Executive Success in the Face of Adversity*. Rocklin, CA: Forum.

Iacocca, L., & Novak, W. (1984). *Iacocca: An Autobiography*. Toronto: Bantam Books.

Jenson, R. (2001). *Achieving Authentic Success*. San Diego: Future Achievement International.

Kouzes, J.M., & Posner, B.Z. (1999). *Encouraging the Heart: A Leader's Guide to Rewarding and Recognizing Others*. San Francisco: Jossey-Bass.

Kouzes, J.M., & Posner, B.Z. (2008). *The Leadership Challenge*, (4th ed.). San Francisco: Jossey-Bass.

Kytle, C. (1969). *Ghandi: Soldier of Nonviolence*. Washington, DC: Seven Locks Press.

Lardner, J. (1999). World-class Workaholics. *U.S. News & World Report*. (December 20, 1999).

Lencioni, P. (2000). *The Four Obsessions of an Extraordinary Executive*. San Francisco: Jossey-Bass.

Lencioni, P. (2002). *The Five Dysfunctions of a Team: A Leadership Fable*. San Francisco: Jossey-Bass.

Malcomson, R. (2006). *Historical Dictionary of the War of 1812*. Lanham, Maryland: The Scarecrow Press.

Manchester, W. (1983). *Winston Spencer Churchill: The Last Lion, Visions of Glory, 1874-1932*. New York: Dell Publishing.

Markham, F. (1963). *Napoleon*. New York: New American Library.

McCullough, D. (1992). *Truman*. New York: Touchstone.

McCullough, D. (2001). *John Adams*. New York: Simon & Schuster.

McCullough, D. (2005). *1776*. New York: Simon & Schuster.

Murray, I.H. (1987). *Jonathan Edwards: A New Biography*. Edinburgh: Banner of Truth Trust.

Raines, C. (2003). *Connecting Generations: The Sourcebook for a New Workplace.* Menlo Park, CA: Crisp Publications.

Reagan, R. (1990). *Ronald Reagan: An American Life.* New York: Pocket Books.

Senge, P.M. (1994). *The Fifth Discipline: The Art and Practice of the Learning Organization.* New York: Currency/Doubleday.

Schwarzkopf, H.N., & Petre, P. (1992). *It Doesn't Take a Hero.* New York: Bantam Books.

Smith, D.M. (2008). *Divide or conquer: How Great Teams Turn conflict into Strength.* New York: Portfolio.

Stewart, J.B. (2006). *Disney War.* New York: Simon and Schuster.

Sullivan, G.R., & Harper, M.V. (1996). *Hope is Not a Method: What Business Leaders Can Learn from America's Army.* New York: Broadway Books.

Swenson, R.A. (1992). *Margin: Restoring Emotional, Physical, Financial, and Time Reserves to Overloaded Lives.* Colorado Springs: Navpress.

Thatcher, M. (1993). *Margaret Thatcher: The Downing Street Years.* New York: HarperCollins.

Wilke, S., & Wilke, R. (2010). *The Leading Edge: 9 Strategies for Improving Internal and Intentional Leadership.* San Diego: LEADon, Inc.

Wives of the Signers: The Women Behind the Declaration of Independence. (2010). Aledo, Texas: WallBuilder Press.

Zemke, R., Raines, C., & Filipczak, B. (2000). *Generations at Work: Managing the Clash Of Veterans, Boomers, Xers, and Nexters in Your Workplace.* New York: American Management Association.